FITNESS   RELATIONSHIPS   EMOTIONS   FINANCES   APPEARANCE   FAITH

# RESET

## 6 ESSENTIAL RESETS TO A HEALTHIER HAPPIER YOU

CELEBRITY MAKEUP ARTIST

# JACQUI PHILLIPS

ISBN (color print): 978-0-9994550-0-5

ISBN (greyscale print): 978-0-9994550-2-9

ISBN (kindle): 978-0-9994550-1-2

Library of Congress Control Number (LCCN): 2017955711

Cover Photography by Matt Peyton for Matt Peyton Photography

Cover and Interior Hair and Makeup by Laura Koski for Doll Cosmetics

Photography for Chapter 8 by Chris Elia Luppo

Illustrations concepts and artwork by Jacqui Phillips, graphic design of illustrations completed by Lika Kvirikashvii and Dilan Perera

Editing Contributions by Chris Elia Luppo

Additional Editing Consultation by Wendy K. Walters

Prepared for Publication By

Palm Tree Publications is a Division of Palm Tree Productions
www.palmtreeproductions.com
PO BOX 122 | KELLER, TX | 76244

*Unless otherwise noted, Scriptures were taken from THE HOLY BIBLE, NEW INTERNATIONAL VERSION®, NIV® Copyright © 1973, 1978, 1984, 2011 by Biblica, Inc.® Used by permission. All rights reserved worldwide.*

To Contact the Author:

**www.JacquiPhillips.tv**

*I would like to dedicate this to God for using me to write this book. You have humbled my heart and changed my life forever! Thank You for loving me enough and trusting me to do this. I am in awe of all that You have done, are doing, and excited for what is to come. Thank You with my sincerest eternal gratitude! I love You with all my heart and more than words can say ... but You know that!*

# I'd Like To Thank ...

## Mom and Dad

I love you with all my heart. You are my everything. We have all been through so much together and have come out of it all with love and more love. I thank you for all that you have taught me, and for all that you have done to make my life better. I love you both and I am so grateful that you are my parents as I am so inspired by you!

## Grandma

Thank you for loving me the way you did. I love you with my entire heart! You were my angel on earth and I miss you every single day.

## PapPap

Thank you for all our beautiful and fun moments! Thank you for teaching me the power of love and showing me that we are only physically separated by death, but we are always together. This lesson forever changed my life and I have never once questioned my faith thanks to you!

# Judy Collins

Thank you for all the gifts you have given me in my lifetime. You have been one of my greatest teachers and are a true angel and a Godsend. I am forever grateful for you, for your inspiration, and for all that you have done for me. I would not be who I am today if it wasn't for you. You have touched my life in a way that changed me forever. You have shown me the world and taught me about every spectrum of media, but most importantly how to constantly strive to be a better person. I love and cherish you with all my heart as our friendship was a divine appointment. I am so grateful to God for You!

# Wendy Walters

First of all, thank you for even taking on this project. I wasn't even sure I was going to ever write a book, but you kept encouraging me that I had many books in me. Thanks to your encouragement and showing me the way, I believed you—and now look at all the books I have written during the time I wrote this one! There is no explanation for us meeting other than God. When he puts the desire in your heart, He will make a way for it to happen and you were that way! You are an angel and helped me bring this to life better than I could ever have imagined. Thank you for listening to me, caring about this project the way I do, and for sharing your beautiful divine gifts with me and my RESET! I am so honored to work with you —this has been a wonderful surprise and the definition of a divine moment. I love you more than words can say. Thank you for your excellence and your beautiful team that brought this to the finish line. May God bless all you do and continue to surprise us with these beautiful moments. Thank you my beautiful friend with a beautiful soul ... I love you forever!

# John Luppo

Thank you for being the brother I never had but always needed. I can truly look back on the last five years of my life and see that you have had a hand in every good and godly opportunity, friendship, and experience. I can never thank you enough in words as I am so grateful for our friendship. Thank you for helping me strengthen my relationship with God and believing in me to keep pushing me forward. You are an example of why we should answer our call as you have helped to change my life forever and I am blessed to call you my friend. Thank you my brother!

# Chris Elia Luppo

Thank you for being such a wonderful sister, friend, mentor and encourager. I truly can never thank you enough for all you have done in my life. Thank you for all the time and effort you have taken to sow into me. Thank you for sharing all your knowledge, expertise and gifts with me. Thank you for spending the entire summer editing my book with me. You are truly a Godsend and I can never thank you enough for answering this call to help me as I so needed you and I am so thankful for you, your love, and our beautiful friendship. God bless you. Thank you. I love and adore you!

# Laura Koski

You are my sister and best friend. I love you more than words can say and I am forever grateful for our lifelong friendship. Thank you for always supporting me, loving me, and never judging me. Thank you for always providing me a safe place to go when I needed to seek help and listening with love. Thank you for all your hard work in helping me with this book, my projects, and for always having so many genius ideas. Thank you for sharing your gifts with me in designing my look for this cover. I love you with all my heart!

## Pastor Veryl Howard

Thank you for coming into my life and being such a guiding force in strengthening my walk with God. I am forever grateful for our divine appointment and for you being my Spiritual Mama. Thank you for believing in me, loving me, and taking the time to teach me and show me all that I needed to learn in entertainment. I am a better person because of you and my walk with God is so much stronger because of your guidance and influence through the years. I love you with all my heart!

## The Mobwives

To my beautiful sweet friends from *Mobwives*: Renee Graziano, Carla Facciolo, and Karen Gravano, I love you with all my heart! You have all been through both RESETs with me and encouraged me with unconditional love, strength, and kindness. Watching you all transform with such tenacity and courage in front of my eyes no matter what was in front of you encouraged and inspired me beyond words. I truly can never thank you enough for all the support you have showed. You are family to me and I love you!

## Sifu Karl Romain

Thank you for being such a magnificent co-host, business partner, and friend. You are the other brother I never had but always needed. Thank you for sharing all your gifts, always encouraging me, and being the

first one in line to help. Your friendship has been a divine appointment that I am forever grateful for. God bless you my dear friend, I love you very much!

## Lorraine Pascale

Our friendship is a divine appointment. You are an angel in my life and I am forever grateful for it. You are a beautiful, kind, and loving soul. Thank you for sharing your many gifts with me. You are a great teacher in my life and the sister I never had but always needed. I love you very much!

## Boomer Esiason

Thank you for encouraging me on a daily basis to continue to RESET my health. Thank you for all your support, and sharing your great knowledge with me. I am so grateful for the wonderful years of working with you on your show as it has been one of my greatest gifts during my RESET. It really provided the discipline I needed. I am forever grateful, thank you!

## Jessica Totaro Diktas

Thank you for being such a beautiful soul sister. Thank you for all that you have taught me in the power of meditation, mindfulness, and yoga. You have changed my life for the better. I am forever grateful to you and thankful that God brought you into my life. I love you my sweet friend. I am a better person and definitely a more balanced one because of your influence. Thank you!

# Darryl Strawberry

Thank you, Darryl, for being such an inspiration in my life. I have learned a lot from you about strengthening my walk with God and I am grateful. You are a bright light shining in the world with so many gifts that you generously share, I am honored you had the kindness to endorse my book. Thank you and may God bless you always!

# Ambujam Laksmi

Thank you for being such a beautiful friend and teacher in my life. You have taught me so much about loving myself and learning to listen to my discernment. Thank you for all the beautiful gifts you have given me to tap into. I am forever changed because of you. I love you very much, thank you!

# Matt Peyton

Thank you from my entire heart for being so generous with your genius gifts of photography, creativity, and vision. My dream for this moment was to shoot in a beautiful studio in NYC with you—a renowned photographer! You made my dream come true and I am grateful. Thank you for taking the time and for all your hard work in producing this magical cover. God bless and I love you my friend!

# Lynn Fitch

Thank you for being such a beautiful soul and tremendous influence in my life. I am who I am so much today because of you and all that you taught and showed me. I love you with all my heart and I am grateful that God brought you into my life when He did. You will always have a very special place in my heart. I love you very much!

# George Buitrago & Thomas Patteson
## Body Culture

Thank you for all your motivation, positive reinforcement, and constant encouragement that I can RESET my body and my life! I could not have done it without you. I am grateful and so thankful that I found the courage to keep trying. Thank you for all that you have taught me about fitness and learning to love and listen to my body. Your company and you are both Godsends. Thank you for everything ... I love you both. You rock!

# Chazz Palminteri

Chazz Palminteri you are such an inspiration in my life. You have taught me so much about entertainment and the pursuit of great success! You have instilled in me never to give up, that it is never too late and that if you really believe in something in your soul to go for it all the way! Thank you for being an Angel in my life! There were so many times that you helped me that you didn't even realize it and I will never forget it! You are the definition of kindness and I am so grateful for your friendship and great influence that you and your beautiful wife Gianna have had in my life! I love you both very much! God Bless You always and may you continue to shine your light and greatness with the world!

# Lisa Ascolese

Thank you for being a light in my life and for your constant inspiration and encouragement! I love and adore you! Thank you for including me in your wonderful non profit AOWIE as you have been a positive force in showing me that we can in fact make our dreams come true. I love you my sweet friend!

## Aleida Irizarry & Ashleigh Williams

Thank you for being with me every step of the way on my RESET journey. Your constant encouragement, love, support, and friendship mean the world to me. You really have been my rock and I love you both with all my heart!

## Christian Women In Media Association
### CWIMA

Thank you for the beautiful support you provide and for all the encouragement that all of you lovely ladies give on a daily basis. I am honored to be a part of and a leader in such a distinct group of women who all share our faith in God. Thank you for believing in me and sowing so much good into my life. I love you all!

## Master Media Group

I am truly honored to be a part of your beautiful group and our meetings are truly life changing. Thank you for inviting me to join you and for all the support and encouragement you offer as you are all a blessing. I love you all!

## Trinity Broadcast Network
### TBN

Thank you for the opportunity to host *Joy In Our Town* on your network for so many years. It is an honor and a privilege and my life is forever changed because of it. I am eternally grateful. God bless you all!

# Warren Woodberry

Thank you for having so much faith in me as a host for your *Millenium Magazine.* I am so appreciative for all the tremendous opportunities you give me. I am so honored to be a part of such a wonderful publication and I am forever grateful!

# Global Simmons Group & In Joy Life Center

Thank you for giving me the courage and inspiration to believe in myself and to share my faith with the world. I am filled with the sincerest gratitude for all that you have done in my life. May God bless you for all the good you do in the world. Thank you and I love you all!

# Dr. Terrell Jenkins

Thank you for believing in me and helping me start my Prison Ministry. You have been a divine appointment in my life and I am deeply changed because of it. Thank you for constantly encouraging me and helping me to make my dreams come true. May God continue to bless the great anointing you have over your life as you are a blessing to so many. Thank you my friend, and much love and blessings to you always!

# Victoria Pressly & Frank Cipolla

Thank you for all the wonderful media opportunities that you present to me. I am grateful!

## Lucky Gallimier

Thank you from my entire heart for all the beautiful designs you create and share with me. You are a jewel in the world that is shining bright and I am so grateful to you for all you do. You are an angel!

## Jacob Bressers

Thank you for being a shining example of what RESET is all about. Thank you for being so courageous and sharing your beautiful spirit with me. Thank you for your fierce encouragement, I love you very much!

## Lika Koirikashvilli

Thank you for your beautiful illustrations, sharing your gifts with me, and making my vision and drawings come to life. You were a life saver and I am so grateful for you. Thank you and God bless you from my entire heart!

## Dylan Perera

Thank you for your beautiful illustrations and making my vision come to life. I am so grateful for you. May God bless you and your beautiful gifts that you so generously shared with me for my many projects. Thank you!

## My Family & Friends

Thank you for always loving me and encouraging me. Thank you for all the lessons I have learned along the way as they made me a better person. Thank you for the unconditional love I have always received. May God bless each and every one of you. I love you with all I am!

# Praise For RESET

In her book, *RESET*, Jacqueline Phillips proves that it's never too late to reset your life and find the happiness you always wanted.

*Chazz Palminteri*
*Academy Award Nominated Actor, Director, Writer, Restauranteur*

*RESET* is a book that gives you hope and encouragement that it is never too late to start over. It allows you to realize that God never gives up on you.

*Darryl Strawberry*
*Former Major League Baseball Player*
*4 World Series Titles, 8 Time National League All-Star, Rookie Of The Year*

Jacqui Phillips had been a *Millennium Magazine* host for a few years now and has been a shining example of what a brand ambassador represents for an organization. Each encounter with Jacqui is a welcomed one, for she is always positive, full of energy, and offers words of encouragement that stay with you throughout the day. She is a team player, a go-getter, and in your corner as your biggest supporter when you need her. Jacqui is an example of what her book *RESET* is all about as she is living proof that we can all change our lives to make a positive impact. *RESET* is a must read as you too can turn your pain to purpose!

*Warren Woodberry*
*Publisher, Millenium Magazine*

*RESET* is an amazing and inspiring book for all walks of life. This book touches every and any soul who walks this earth. Not only is *RESET* an inspiration, but also a how to book for anyone suffering on any level inside. Jacqui shows you how to find your own light and be your own kind of superhero.

*Jessica Ditkas*
*Author of* The Science and Practice of Mindfulness *Curriculum for Teens*
*Owner of Soul In Motion Yoga*
*Deisigner of Mindfulscents Jewlery*

About a year I was at a very dark point in my life. A lot of changes were happening and I felt lost on so many levels. I was "functional, but not fulfilled." I was a victim of myself. By the grace of God I connected with Jacqui through work and she introduced me to *RESET*. My life will never be the same. She taught me to make myself a priority. She taught me the importance of hard work. And most importantly, she taught me how to love myself. Since my *RESET* I have lost 45 pounds and I have never been healthier or happier. I have found my purpose and path once again. *RESET* is so much more than just a book, it is a beacon of truth and light. It has changed my life—and in many ways, saved it. I am forever grateful for Jacqui and can only hope that *RESET* reaches the hands of millions. We all could benefit from it.

*Jacob John Bressers*
*Celebrity Personal Assistant*

Jacqui Phillips is not only inspirational, but a living testimony to a life transformed. In her fabulous new book you will see a woman who is transparent and has faced real challenges and overcome them brilliantly. Jacqui gives step-by-step advice on how you can *RESET* any area of your life. You will be encouraged and inspired to reach for your dreams. Her smile, kindness, and caring for others makes her shine brightly like the star she is.

*Chris and John Lippo*
*TV Producers, Filmmakers, and Ministers*

I am very proud of Jacqui and all her accomplishments ... no matter what she went through in life, she always put on a brave face and a beautiful smile. She always put others first—something I admire about her. She is a great friend and a strong woman who never let anyone get in the way of her dreams. *RESET* is a testimony to a life well lived.

*Karen Gravano*
*NY Times Best Selling Author of* MobDaughter
*Reality Star of Mobwives*
*Entrepreneur*

I am so honored to be a part of this beautiful baby, *RESET.* When I read Jacqui's story, I was like a proud momma watching her blossom. From the time I first met her by accident on a plane, I knew that there was much inside her waiting to come out. I have watched her journey and can testify that her raw, honest, heartfelt words will testify to so many.

People need to know they do not have to drown and fail in their finances, relationship, purpose, and more. Jacqui inspires them by being a living example of an overcomer. The six principles she shares are epic with respect to starting over in life. Her faith in God caused her to soar and see the woman God made her to be.

Jacqui's candidness is a bondage-breaker for those blessed to read this book. The Bible says in Romans 8:28 (KJV): *"And we know that all things work together for good to them that love God, to them who are the called according to His purpose."*

She took a messed up situation and birthed life! As you read *RESET,* you will discover that you have purpose, you have power, you have promise, and you have God's hands on you!

*Pastor Veryl Howard*
*Jacqui's Spiritual Mom & Mentor*
*Celebrity Gospel Manager*

*RESET* is an empowering and loving book that helps to elicit the confidence, breath, and strength we all need to muster up to move beyond heartbreak, sadness, and disappointments. This book is filled with warm words and truths through *RESET*. Jacqui Phillips is truly an inspiration to everyone who is blessed enough to know her—a leader and a trail blazer. We all need to take the time to *RESET* our days and our lives.

*Lisa Ascolese*
*www.inventingatoz.com*

Jacqui Phillips is not only a motivational speaker, but also an inspiration to many women. She is a living testimony to how a life can be transformed FOR THE BETTER. In her fabulous new book, *RESET*, you will see a woman who is transparent, who faced real challenges and overcame them brilliantly. Jacqui gives you step-by-step advice on how you can *RESET* any area of your life. You will be encouraged and inspired to reach for your dreams. Her smile, kindness, and caring for others makes her shine brightly like the star she is.

On a personal note, Jacqui Phillips is the definition of GODS CHILD AT WORK—a real living angel who has seen me through the worst of the worst in my life. Her heartfelt words weren't just words to me, they were almost Gospel to me while I danced very intimately with the devil ... I kid you not. She doesn't even know how many times her voice and genuine words of love and light would lead me back to the right side of the tracks. To this day she's my go to when the going gets me wanting to go go go! Not everyone has a close friend like Jacqui Phillips in their life ... but when you read *RESET*, you will have the next best thing!

*Renee Graziano*
*Author, Reality Star, Executive Producer, Entreprreneur*

I am so proud of my friend Jacqui Phillips! I originally met Jacqui on the set of VH1's *Mobwives*. She was our makeup artist and the sweetest girl I have ever worked with! Through all her ups and downs, Jacqui always had a smile on her face. She is one of the strongest and smartest women I know. Her story of *RESET* is inspiring.

*Carla Facciolo*
*Reality Star of VH1 Mobwives*
*Entrepreneur, Creator Of Facciolo Wines*

I can't wait to get this book in the hands of a few friends. Jacqui is such a kind soul and this *RESET* approach is a refreshing way to look within and renew the you that you already know is there. I will be going back to this book over and over again!

*Ashley Williams*
*Celebrity Makeup Artist*

Jacqui Phillips is an amazing co-host and friend. Her book *RESET* is honest, vulnerable, and transformative. It is filled with relatable stories about her life. In her own unique way, Jacqui shares great ideas on how you can reinvent, reset, and restore your life to be the life of your dreams. This book will be your solution to the challenges life brings your way in your relationships, fitness, appearance, emotions, finance, and faith.

*Sifu Romain*
*Certified Master Coach, Martial Arts World Champion, Best Selling Author*

If things are not going the way you want in life and there are changes you know you need to make, Jacqui's empowering book *RESET* is a must-buy book. It will help you live the life of your dreams!

*Lorraine Pascale*
*Sunday Times Best Selling Author, TV Chef, Philanthropist*

As a Personal Development Coach, I couldn't stop reading *RESET.* This book allows you to understand the importance of using your own uniqueness to create an amazing life. Jacqui has a way of taking a complex subject and making it easy so that you can take action and see results immediately. It's a must read and I recommend it to all my clients.

*Thomas Patterson*
*Personal Development Coach*
*Co-Owner of Body Culture*

When I met Jacqui, she expressed to me the hardships she experienced in her life and how she overcame them. She also told me how she wanted to put her formula into words that would help the next person overcome any hardship they may experience. The result is this book you hold in your hands.

I have no doubt in my mind, that once you read *RESET* you will find yourself inspired, motivated, and willing to take greater risk to become closer to your goals. Her mission is simply to get others to follow their dreams.

I have known Jacqui for a great deal of time. I have nothing but the utmost, kind, dearest, caring words to say about her. Jacqui is the kind of person who comes into your life and you do all you can to keep her around for an eternity. She opens doors, creates opportunities, and champions all the right causes.

There is no greater time to reset than at this very moment. This book is more than words, it's more than a message—it's an energy. It is something we all need when we are not feeling strong enough.

*Lucky Galimier*
*Creator & Designer*
*Fashion House of Galimier*
*Paris, France*

# Contents

# Foreword by Judy Collins

Jacqui Phillips has written a new book that is a must have in this time of stress or pressure. *RESET* will answer the need to find a way to cut to the chase and really get going with your life. Jacqui takes you through the needed steps to find your way to freedom and a new way at looking at where you are and where you want to be. She shows you how to become the warrior of your own changes, a champion for your own inner peace and beauty. She shows you how to step into your own joy and live a happy, healthy, light-filled life—a RESET. I love this book!

*Judy Collins*
*Singer, author, songwriter*

# Author's Note Concerning Judy Collins

I met Judy Collins shortly after my grandmother died. I had just started working in entertainment and I knew meeting Judy was a gift from my grandmother and from God above. She taught me everything about the entertainment industry and showed me the way.

As her makeup artist, Judy took me around the world with her. She taught me how to travel and live on the road. She inspired me to write and have the courage to share whatever gifts I have with the world. She taught me to always try my hardest and give my best no matter how I felt and no matter the odds. She always said the "try" was worth it.

I am forever changed because of my relationship with this beautiful woman and I am always grateful to her for being such a beacon of light, love, and hope in my life. Judy is an angel and to me she has been my everything! I love her with all my heart. I was deeply honored when she agreed to write the foreword to my book.

# Preface

Just like yours, my life has been a series of trials and victories, and errors and achievements. Everyone says they can offer you a blueprint and that is great, but I think there is a missing link. In this book, *RESET*, I'm offering you some tools I used that worked for me and the opportunity to dig deep into yourself and look to God for that person that you desire to be. God made us all unique. Use your uniqueness as the starting point to go after your dreams!

As you read I want you to listen to your heart and soul and identify what is unique about you and define the steps you need to make next on your journey of discovery. I hope this book helps you to realize the power that resonates in you. I hope it helps you find your "why" and you will certainly learn to fly!

My message that I want to share with you from my personal experience is not to let people steal your youth, your joy, or your dreams! I want you to find the power to own it all outright, and if you don't to take it back.

This book will lead you to find the courage to break the shackles that have you trapped and bring you to your freedom. Whether you are twenty or seventy years old, if you are alive then you still have time to change your life, to chase your dreams. My dream was to inspire people to aspire. I realized this as I was meandering through my purpose. My search turned to vision, which turned to a direct calling to do what I knew best: beauty, tv/media, and writing from my heart. I hope when you read RESET you can feel my passion and receive the motivation I long and pray for you to have. I am rooting for you, now it's time for you to root for yourself!

# RESET Categories

Together we will work through several areas where you might need a RESET. In each category I share my struggles—real and raw with no gloss or cover-ups. I came to understand that my life was like a tree. Each branch represented a different category of my well being. These categories are:

- Health & Fitness

- Relationships,

- Emotions

- Finances

- Appearance

- Faith

Whatever I watered grew and whatever I neglected died. If your life was reflected on the branches of this tree, what would that mean? What story would be told?

**Tree of Life**

Health
Fitness

Appearance

Emotions

Finances

Relationships

Faith

**Whatever you
water will grow**

**Whatever you
neglect will die**

*Love*

## Disclaimer

What follows is my story. It is how I remember what I went through. As I tell it, know that I love each person involved. I aspire to live in love, grace, and forgiveness. I do not intend or desire to defame anyone's character. We all have the right to make choices. My choices to stay in bad circumstances were mine. Now in hindsight I am able to look back and accept these responsibilities. Some people in my life did some bad things. I have done some bad things, but I chose to walk away from the bad things. So with that being said, all of you

beautiful people reading this book have a choice to make. The choice is yours. What will you choose? What choices will you make to better your life and step into your truth? If you find your "why" then you will fly. To do that you must **FLY**:

First
Love
Yourself

-JJ

In the pages which follow, I am going to be vulnerable. I am about to share things with you that were painful to experience and are embarrassing to admit. I do it so that someone else who is where I was can flip on the light switch earlier than I did. I stayed in the dark too long. I want others who feel trapped like I did to leave their dark place and step into the beautiful sunlight. I share my pain to help someone else find a way out of theirs.

## Chapter One

# WHEN LOVE IS NOT ENOUGH

*"Get rid of unnecessary aggravation. If you are going jump off the diving board, first you need a clean pool."*

—JJ

Today I woke up screaming. It was as if the lion in me woke up after many years of sleeping and was screaming for its everlasting life. A voice on the inside shook my spirit and shouted, "Come on, you're slowly dying! What the heck is wrong with you?" I woke up screaming, but nothing came out. Although a lion was loudly roaring on the inside of me, the room was deadly quiet.

I knew this was the first day of the rest of my life. I was finding my old self, but creating a better version of her. I wasn't exactly sure where to start, but I knew it was time.

"If you get your body back," I thought, "you will get your mind back and all the weight will fall off."

I knew this wasn't figuratively speaking, I literally meant that all the weight I was physically and spiritually carrying was a true reflection

and mirror image of my psyche. I was carrying the pounds of emotional turmoil. Here I was at a pivotal point in my life and totally unhappy. Almost every area of my life was a disaster.

"How did I let it get this far?" I wondered, "How could I do this to myself?"

I had always loved myself enough to watch out for me. My goodness, as an only child I had no choice! If I didn't have my own back who did? The most disturbing question I kept asking myself and getting the same answer was this, "What do I do when love is not enough? What do people do when love is not enough? What do you do when you have invested over a decade of your life with someone and you know the only future waiting for you is filled with unhappiness, disappointment and maybe death?"

It was a shocking realization. It was why the lion inside was screaming for me to wake up. I had always been an athlete, so instinctively I knew I needed to work out my body to work out my mind. I thought, "If I get my brain right, my answers will come." I had to let the chips fall where they may. I needed to shed more than pounds, I needed to shed some people! I had to get the negative out of my life, it was weighing me down. I needed to plow away a pathway to light! I needed to create a walkway to follow. I knew it would be a lot of steps, a lot of long strides, but I had a newfound awareness. I knew each stride would be poignant, and I would need to remember it in order to learn. Most importantly, that roaring lion woke me up to the fact that I wasn't living the life God had intended for me at all!

> *That roaring lion woke me up ... I wasn't living the life God intended for me*

When your lion roars ...

listen!

I decided the life I was living wasn't how I wanted to live. I laid in bed, in the stillness of fresh awareness, and decided what I wanted my life to look like. I determined how to make the steps needed to make a change. I started to ask myself some questions:

- What was I like when I was the most happy?

- At what age was this?

- What did I do then? (what activities, etc.)

- What was my body like?

- What did I eat?

- Did I drink alcohol?

After I started to answer these questions for myself, I got very depressed and perplexed. Even though I felt overwhelmed, I decided to start my plan of attack right away. If not I knew I would die … and soon! In fact, part of me wanted to die, it would be easier than facing that long road ahead of me. I felt really desperate, like the good part of me was dying. That there was this distorted shell of me and it was awful, ugly, and sad.

"It's time for a RESET," I said out loud.

I needed to reset my happiness button. Forget that, because first I needed to find my happiness button! I started to envision the times I felt happiest (or somewhat happy at this point), let's be real this was a sad state of affairs. I knew I needed to formulate a way to obtain a new me. My new me was simply the old me—just the girl I used to be before life got too messy.

"Who was I before the world told me who to be?"

"Who was I before life got in the way of my joy?"

"It's my fault though. All of it!" I thought, "You were never strong enough to say no."

It was true. I had always put others before me. The old me was the kind of girl that did not let grass grow under her feet, and she kept her feet moving. She knew how to do what she wanted when she wanted it. Old "Jacqui" simply did it. I wanted to be her again. I wanted her youthful spirit, without the ton of bricks I felt around my neck—like I was drowning. I felt like I had a piano on my chest and I was slowly and strongly sinking into the ground. It was loose ground, like quicksand. I thought, "If I did not do something and take action, at least one step, well then I will die!"

My mom kept telling me the same thing. "JJ," I could hear her voice (JJ is what my family calls me), "You are going to get sick you are going to have a heart attack. You could get cancer … you could have a stroke! It's not good to be this angry and stressed all the time. It is so unhealthy!"

It was like she was in the room with me, adding her voice to that lion. "I know you are not happy," she would say, "and not because you are overweight. You are overweight because you are not happy and your body is reacting to your emotions. You are too good for this! Please help yourself!"

I could hear my dad chiming in too, "JJ, just walk away. Leave everything! Who cares? Come home. Start over!"

I remembered all my arguments, "Dad," I would say, "I have responsibilities, I want to come home but the banks trusted me enough to lend me this money for a mortgage and for my business, so I am not going to be a degenerate and not hold up my end of the bargain! It's just not right. It is not who I am! But thank you and I love you!"

I sat up in bed. "Let's go!" I said out loud.

Sometime that November, I got an email from Daily Candy for a bootcamp kickboxing special. I thought to myself, "This is exactly what I need … to kick something!"

So I texted my friend to see if she wanted to do it with me. She said, "Come to my gym with me, I have free passes. This will change your life!" … and it did.

*"People show you who they are. Believe them."*
—Maya Angelou

# Think About It

- ❧ Who are you?

- ❧ What has happened to you?

- ❧ Where are you in life?

- ❧ Where do you want to go?

- ❧ Do you love yourself, and if not, why?

Before we continue to completely abuse ourselves any longer, let's figure out what is working and what isn't working.

For instance, in my life at this moment, I am lucky to have a great career going. I am a professional makeup artist, so I am fortunate that I can fake my looks because of the gifts and skills that God gave me. But let's face it I AM A HOT MESS RIGHT NOW!

I may not be as grateful for it as I should be, but thankfully I make a great living. I can support myself and can financially depend on myself. Unfortunately, I'm financially supporting everything in my life

which includes my boyfriend, businesses, home, cars, insurance etc… and it is overwhelming. I feel like I have an elephant on my chest. The stress is unbearable. So, it's official … I can not breathe! I AM SUFFOCATING!

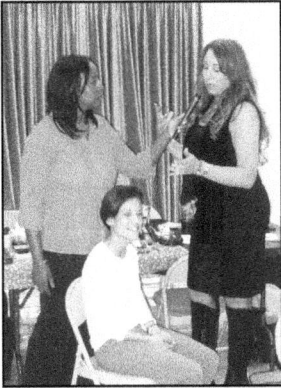

I mean this picture of me on Valerie Persaud's TV show is the proof in the pudding. I have not one, but two pairs of Spanx on … and I still look FAT! Under my smile and my fake hair (yes, I have extensions in), my fake tan, and my fake lashes there is a very scared, upset, disappointed girl. Today she finally woke up and realized that her life is a nightmare!

Thank God I was able to change all this … and I am going to show you how!

As a Celebrity Makeup Artist, I have learned how to focus on a person's best attributes when I am getting them camera ready. So I decided I would do that for myself. I know it's smart to highlight your best features, highlight your strengths, and build from there. If you have attributes—whether it be your mind, body, or your spiritual strength—it's empowering to focus on these. Start there and grow and nurture from the strengths you already have.

"*With strength comes wisdom, with wisdom comes purpose, with purpose comes peace, with peace comes love.*"

—JJ

# Chapter Two

# Mirror, Mirror

*"Before you can create a fresh face, you first need to take all the makeup off."*

-JJ

## Who is that staring back at me?

B efore I could even begin to get back to where I needed to be, I first had to ask myself the question, "How did I get here?" I needed to assess what had happened, what had gone wrong in my life to get me to this point?

All of a sudden I woke up in this body and didn't recognize it anymore. I sat in this moment in time, trapped in a traumatic life situation. It wasn't

cancer. I didn't have a tragic accident or suffer the loss of a loved one, but it was trauma. I was a stranger to myself and it was completely and utterly mind blowing! "Where was God?" I wondered. I had certainly been talking to God, but it felt like God had forgotten about me ... or did I just simply quit listening? I sighed deeply, depression closing the walls in around me, "How could all this be happening?"

If I was confronting only one situation at a time, I could have handled it. But I was facing several problems simultaneously and it was overwhelming. It felt like I had no way out—no way through that led me to a happier outcome. I thought the pressure would kill me, and maybe part of me kind of wanted to die. I wasn't sure if I really meant it, but a nice long sleep to avoid this drama sure seemed like it would bring great relief. At least for now.

Here is what I was facing:

- The business I had started abruptly ended. I was in a bad partnership and they had their own bankruptcy issues. It felt like the last seven years of my life had been an absolute, complete waste. I had nothing to show for the investment but loss!

- My boyfriend (at the time) was also a business partner. Because of the business, we were in debt to the tune of $256,852.36. If you subtracted the mortgage it was $95,852.36 ... but debt is debt and it was crushing. I say "we" were in debt, but in the end, it was only me responsible for it all. Even though his name was on one or two things, all the debt was incurred against my social security number, all credit was based on my personal income. I was the responsible party, and I was the one who made each and every one of the payments.

- I was 40 pounds overweight. I was officially fat! I had been lean and athletic my entire life, but now for the first time in my life I was fat. Not chubby. Not curvy. I was fat. The girl looking back at me in the mirror had lost herself—lost her self esteem. The weight I carried was far heavier than extra pounds, it was spiritual weight and it was crushing me!

- I spent too many years in a relationship that wasn't leading to a long-term future. Though I loved him, we did not belong together anymore. I had wasted my youth on a possible future with this person—and it was definitely was not leading to marriage and the family I desired.

- I had never married and I did not have children. My biological clock was ticking loudly in my subconscious. Deep disappointment was stirring. I felt old, washed up and the dream of having a family felt like it was completely over.

- I felt trapped on a hamster wheel that I did not sign up to ride, but there was no getting off. I owed so much money I had to keep that wheel spinning madly.

- I was terrified I was going to lose all my belongings I worked so hard for. Losing my home, cars, investments … all seemed an inevitable reality.

- I was under so much stress my health was compromised. I literally feared death.

- All my dreams had become nightmares. I was suffocating—drowning not only in my present pain, but in all the pain I knew was to come. I was on a terrible roller coaster and thought, "Can I please cash in my tickets and get off this terrifying ride?"

I had no idea how to make it all stop. No clue how to begin turning it around.

I felt like I was functioning under anesthesia—sleepwalking through my own life. Not really awake, not really aware, just numb to everything.

Was I under anesthesia? Yes! My anesthesia of choice was wine, food, and my very unhealthy codependent relationship. So I ask you, "Are you under anesthesia too? If so what is yours?"

Anesthesia can be anything that leave us functional, but not fulfilled. It can be alcohol, men, sugar, gambling, fitness, tv, shopping … and it can go on and on. These things serve just like anesthesia—a numbing mechanism to avoid the actual pain. Anesthesia helps you sleep through the things that are cutting you open. It just quiets the elephant in the room!

We seek an antidote from pain. All the coping mechanisms we choose to anesthetize ourselves from pain stem from the thoughts in our head, the things we believe about ourselves. Thoughts are so powerful that when we put enough attention on them, when we give them enough of our focus and energy, they manifest in physical form. We think it, and it becomes our reality. A self-fulfilling prophecy.

# Profound and Non-profound Truths

Our lives are made up of profound and non-profound truths. Profound truths are based on facts. These are things that do not change no matter what the circumstances are. Non-profound truths are based on feelings or perceptions—they are the stories we tell ourselves to deal with the circumstance in front of us.

What are your truths, both profound and non-profound? Below are my examples to help you with this first exercise. Please list yours next to mine.

## PROFOUND TRUTHS:
### *Non-negotiable facts about yourself.*

| My Profound Truths | Your Profound Truths |
|---|---|
| *I know there is a God and I love Him.* | |
| *My grandma loved me, I will always love her.* | |
| *I am 5' 9.5" tall.* | |
| *My favorite food is French fries with brown gravy.* | |
| *I am a woman.* | |
| *My parents love me and I love them with all my heart.* | |
| *My eye color is hazel.* | |
| *In order to be happy, I need to work doing things I love.* | |

## NON PROFOUND TRUTHS:
### *The stories in your head that you tell yourself.*

| My Non-Profound Truths | Your Non-Profound Truths |
|---|---|
| *No one loves me.* | |
| *I am ugly and fat.* | |
| *My dreams will never come true.* | |
| *I deserve to be alone.* | |
| *I am in debt.* | |
| *There must be something wrong with me.* | |
| *I am stupid.* | |
| *I will never get married.* | |

At first glance, the difference between these two may seem slight, but they come from a very different thought system. Some of the profound truths are mere facts such as I am 5' 9.5" tall. No matter what I do, this is not going to be altered. Other profound truths such as, my grandma loved me and I will always love her are derived from deeply meaningful experiences. They are facts that I rely on, based on positive experiences.

They have a positive perspective. So indeed they carry a different kind of energy and connotation when reading them. There is definitely a different feeling when I read these words. These profound truths anchor me to a positive place, even if all the "waters of life" surrounding me are trying to convince me otherwise.

Now, the non profound truths are completely different. They are negative and dangerous for any type of growth. A girl who is a size 4 and weighs in at 100 pounds can still tell herself, "I am fat," every single day. She believes this to be true, so it influences her decisions about what she eats, what she wears, and how she presents herself to the world. Her self-esteem is wrapped around a damaging, limiting belief.

For example, when I say to myself, "I will be in debt forever," I cut off my own creativity and resourcefulness to add new streams of income and bring that debt down. I may make a poor impulsive purchase because saying no to one thing doesn't seem like it will have any effect on the bigger problem. Non-profound truths impact the choices you make every single day.

Now lets examine where these truths originate from.

I like illustrations. When I can visualize something, it helps me connect to it more powerfully. It feels more tangible and attainable. It unleashes your imagination. So, throughout the book I will be providing lots of illustrations. I hope they help you as much as they have helped me!

On the next few pages are two family trees. Imagine all these thoughts/spirits I illustrated as people, sitting there on the tree. They are part of your family, your DNA, they make up who you are. They are a part of you and have been passed down to you.

Maybe you learned fear from your environment or a family member. I sure did. It was reinforced by growing up in the restaurant/bar that my family owned, hearing all the very sad stories of some peoples lives.

So imagine Fear as a person, as a member of your family. Once you meet your family member Fear, then Fear introduces you to Lack, then Lack introduces you to Anger ... and so on and so on ... It's a constant flow of negative energy that builds up speed and all of a sudden your life is a big bad tornado—a nightmare!

These thoughts/spirits live in your head. They become real and eventually manifest themselves in physical form. Why? Because when we let them "hang out" with our thoughts, we participate in their destruction and allow that form to be created.

But I have good news! You can wake up from this nightmare. You can literally change the forecast in your mind from harmful tornadoes to sunny skies!

You can hit the STOP/PAUSE button and allow yourself the opportunity to meet and get to know the rest of your family. They live on the other side of your family tree. They are waiting for you. You have met them before, but perhaps you haven't really taken the time to get to know them well. This side of the family has a beautiful member called Love. Love introduces you to Joy, and Joy brings your aunt, Faith. Faith is married to Hope and their child is Peace. They all belong in your family tree too!

Just as Fear, Lack and all their nasty cousins keep you miserable and depressed, Love, Hope and all their cheerful family members make you want to shout for joy! They are wonderful companions, and if you will live with this side of the family long enough, you will want to dump the other side once and for all!

Let me introduce you to the Stronghold Family! These are where your **non-profound truths** derive from. These family members are LACK, CODEPENDENCY, GREED, FEAR, ANGER, JEALOUSY, SELF HATE, and GLUTTONY.

## Stronghold Family Tree

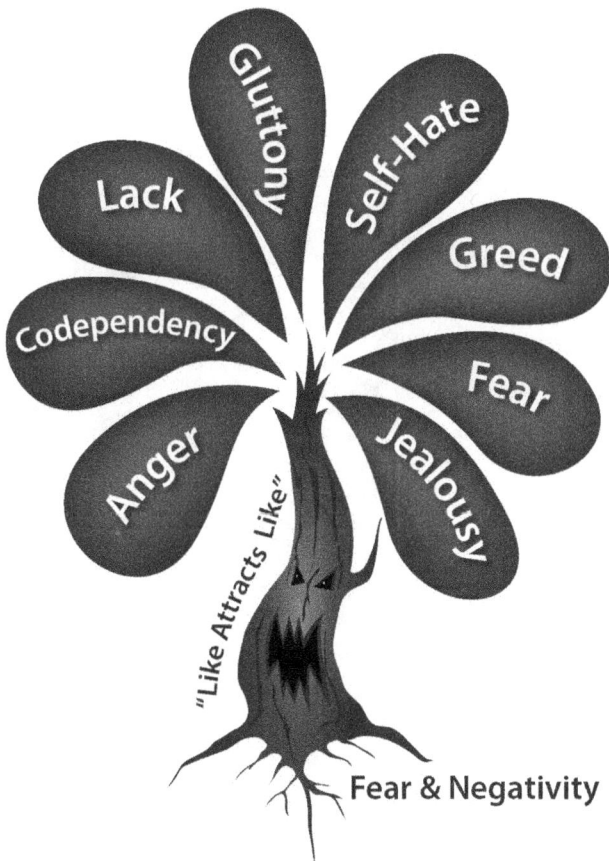

Gluttony

Self-Hate

Lack

Greed

Codependency

Fear

Anger

Jealousy

"Like Attracts Like"

Fear & Negativity

Now allow me introduce you to the Freehold Family! These are where your **profound truths** derive from. These family members are HOPE, FAITH, ABUNDANCE, JOY, GENEROSITY, COURAGE, INTUITION, and BALANCE.

**Freehold Family Tree**

*"And now these three remain: faith, hope, and love. But the greatest of these is love."*

—1 Corinthians 13:13

I woke up one day and realized I was functional, but not fulfilled. I was living, but not living well. I wanted all that to change.

I knew I needed professional help. I was so weak in the areas that were causing my pain I needed some help to regain control, to RESET.

I first started with a bootcamp. I knew if I got my body back I would get my mind back, and then the rest of the bad things would fall off just like the weight. I believed by ridding myself of the excess baggage (not just fat, but also negative people), I would indeed find my spirit.

Bad Finances

Poor Health

Toxic Relationships

Lost Faith

Unhealthy Appearance

Upset Emotions

Weighed Down

I knew I needed to educate myself about the problems that were in my life surrounding it, so I went to a therapist. She really helped me dig deep and see all the darkness surrounding my relationships,

such as the people in my life who were depressed, alcoholics, and the unhealthy and the codependent relationships that I was attracted to and was attracting.

I eventually found another therapist I have now worked with for years who has also been my business coach. I am so grateful for her insight, her loving non-judgmental lessons, and teaching me what accountability is and what it means to me!

# Think About It

Are you functional but not fulfilled? Are you sleepwalking through your life, using outside sources of anesthesia to keep you from feeling (and dealing with) your pain?

Let's reflect. Answer the questions below honestly so you can find out where you are on your journey and figure out what step is next.

- When were you the happiest?

- What were you doing?

- What were you eating?

- Were you drinking alcohol, coffee, soda?

- Who was with you in these moments?

- When were you the saddest?

- What were you doing?

- What were you eating?

- Were you drinking alcohol, coffee, soda?

- Who was with you in these moments?

Trauma is a deeply distressing or disturbing experience. Psychological trauma can occur when something bad has happened to you (like abuse). It can also happen when something good that you needed to happen was absent (like abandonment). Think for a moment about situations that have brought you trauma.

What events or trauma caused you to make the decisions in your life that have led you to where you are now?

What does "normal" look like for you? (A normal relationship with parents, siblings, co-workers, friends, significant other?)

Are you a good friend to yourself? Do you treat yourself well? Do you tell yourself good things or hurtful things inside your mind?

# Eight Attitudes

Eight Attitudes are needed in order for us to embrace a true RESET! Your RESET starts with a new attitude, and I find it imperative to include this now before we go any further so you can keep these in mind as you read and work each chapter. As you must have this in balance in order to maintain any type of healthy relationship—even if only with yourself.

1. **SELF LOVE**

   I am fearfully and wonderfully made. I must embrace who I am with joy and satisfaction. I am enough.

2. **I DESERVE THIS**

   Inspired by the Prayer of Jabez when he," … called on the God of Israel saying, 'Oh, that You would bless me indeed, and enlarge my territory, that Your hand would be with me, and that You

would keep me from evil, that I may not cause pain!' So God granted him what he requested" (1 Chronicles 4:10, NKJV). Yes, I want this!

## 3. SUCCESS

I am not anxious. I expect to succeed. I commit my plans to the Lord and He blesses the work of my hands.

## 4. LEADERSHIP

I will lead myself first. I will seek out others who have success in areas where I want to succeed and allow them to mentor me—even if this is just by their books or teachings. I will lead and be led.

## 5. ACCOUNTABILITY

I will set personal and professional goals and make myself accountable to someone for my progress with those goals.

## 6. OWNERSHIP

I will own my mistakes as well as my successes. I will take responsibility to finish what I start.

## 7. FAITH

My faith guides me. It provides me with a moral code and standards by which I live. I will nourish my faith.

## 8. CHANGE OF MINDSET

My thoughts determine my reality. I will actively examine my thoughts and make sure they are positive, healthy, empowering, and in agreement with my dreams. I will change my mindset whenever I am challenged to think negatively, limit my potential, or be too hard on myself. My thoughts are my responsibility.

## Chapter Three

# I Have the Keys

*"Take off all that mascara so you can see!"*

—JJ

Everything I needed to change was already inside of me. I already had the keys to unlock my shackles, I just needed to figure out how to use them … I needed a RESET!

There were things in my life that I needed serious help with. I had become the "queen of denial"—that dark and twisted road which had taken me so far off the path of happiness and wholeness. I felt so far off course that getting back seemed overwhelming. Where would I start? How would I begin? First, I had to identify what areas most needed a RESET. Because my whole life was in such a mess, I realized that my only hope of success was to pick one area of RESET to focus on, and then chip away at the others one at a time until I found my way back to me.

I identified six major areas where RESET most needed to happen for me. These areas were:

- Health and Fitness

- Relationships

- Emotions

- Finances

- Appearance

- Faith

We have small RESETS every day, little course corrections that help us navigate unexpected things which come up during a normal day. We make these adjustments pretty easily, but a big RESET requires a daily change in our habits, our thoughts, and even in our speech. We have to lock on to a goal—a desired dream for our life, then align our daily choices with that bigger goal. Life has a current, like a river, and it pulls you along the easiest route, taking you where it wills rather than allowing you the choice of destination. But like a salmon swimming upstream to spawn, you too can pursue a chosen destiny, even if it requires that you go against life's current.

Our brain operates according to road maps. The different maps are our neural pathways. As we make choices that become habits, these pathways become like deeply paved, familiar routes to us. The longer we keep the habit, the more certain the route becomes for our brains to make particular decisions to follow. Each day we make choices. When we allow these choices to be guided by emotional responses or as reactions to triggers, these neural pathways grow deeper and more concrete in our brains. Eventually, our decisions become "auto-pilot" responses with no conscious thought.

For example, have you ever driven home from the store and not remembered how you got there? Your brain just knew the way because

it was wired (paved) through years of driving back and forth to the same store. You didn't have to think about it, you went the same way you always did. Habits are just like this. If you have developed healthy habits, then "auto-pilot" takes you to good destinations. However, if your habitual responses are unhealthy or toxic, this same "auto-pilot" feature will cause your life to crash and burn!

> We all have neural networks inside our brains—a system of neurons which talk to each other inside the brain as well as throughout the entire central nervous system. These networks are built by and control what we think, feel, say, and do. They are "wired" together, allowing our neurons to "talk" to each other.
>
> Networks are made up of brain cells (neurons), synapses (the gap between the branchlike extensions of brain cells), neurotransmitters (the chemical messengers), and receptors (receivers of the messages). Together they make "brain maps" or "road maps." These maps help us get through our days efficiently—so we don't have to think about how to brush our teeth or how to read. Once we have learned, it happens automatically, without effort into the thought process.
>
> How long a "road map" has been used, and how many other "road maps" it is connected to determine how strong the "wiring" is within our brain.
>
> These "road maps" go into action as a result of "triggers" that set them into motion. These triggers can be things such as a sight or sound, a touch, a smell, a memory, a person … even a time of day, person, place, color or song can trigger your emotions causing you to think, talk, and act a certain way. We can, however, "rewire" these "maps."[1]

Redemption is possible! You can RESET. There is a way back, but it can only be achieved by taking a different road. We can retrain our brain—rewire, if you will. Incremental changes repeated over time become habits. If the small changes are good ones, they will become healthy habits and these healthy habits will lead to positive outcomes. The small changes can yield big results!

> Thinking affects the entire body. There is mounting scientific evidence demonstrating the intimate relationship between the brain, the rest of the nervous system, the endocrine system, and the immune system ... Because mind controls matter, therefore thinking is the pre-eminent influence on health.[2]

## *"When God looks at me, He sees a warrior. I am a warrior, not a victim!"*

—Lance Wallnau

How I think can change how I actually am! In my soul searching I began to realize that I was not powerless and that I had the power to change—to "rewire" my brain and take back my mind, will, and emotions.

I started by asking myself some tough questions. I invite you to do the same. The following exercise is to help you understand where you are right now and give you the power to change where you will go next. I have given my answers as well, so you can see my process of RESET and hopefully, find strength to complete your own. Awareness and acceptance are the last steps to break denial before your true RESET can begin!

# Worksheet:

## DO YOU FEEL LIKE A VICTIM?

I did. I just could not imagine how my life got this way and how I was ever going to get out of it. I did not sign up for this craziness, but I was living it. I couldn't quite see how the waves of life had swept me up into this mess, but here I was. I was angry, bitter, frustrated, and depressed. Not only did I feel like a victim I felt like a loser. I was too ashamed even to ask for help. I thought I had to get a little bit better first before I could tell anybody about my struggle. I had simply lost my voice.

## WHAT MAKES YOU FEEL TRAPPED?

In my case I felt trapped by my relationship, debt and money responsibilities. I felt like I was in a jail and there was no way out. On top of that, I felt like I was in solitary confinement with no windows—I truly had isolated myself from everyone out of pure embarrassment and because I felt like such a failure I did not see a light at the end of the tunnel. I thought about suicide, but my belief in God held me to take that no further than fantasy. I felt like I was sleep walking through life, trapped with no choices.

## WHAT DO YOU NEED RECOVERY FROM?

I needed to recover from myself! My whole life was a hot mess, but I had to choose where to begin and the first RESET I chose

was my body and health. I knew if I got my body back, I would get my strength back, and then I would get my mind back. I felt like if the physical baggage (excess weight) I was carrying around fell off, the emotional and spiritual weight would fall off with it.

## WHERE DO YOU START THE PROCESS?

I decided to join a fitness bootcamp. I knew I couldn't do this alone and needed some accountability to push me through. I would cry and feel like such a loser. I thought to myself, "My God, how did it get so bad ... I was a great athlete ... how was it possible I could barely do a pushup?" Joining the bootcamp made the RESET decision official. Everyone there was so nice to me, encouraging and affirming. It was the first time I felt like I was doing something good for me in a long time. Other than going to work, I never did anything nice for myself anymore.

*RESET may have to cost you something tangible to prove to you that your decision is real*

The bootcamp cost me more money. Paying for it was part of the process of sacrifice ... and it was worth every dime! Sometimes we need to sacrifice in order to start a real RESET. It has to cost us something tangible so we have proof our decision is real. I still go to the gym. I still pay for this 'babysitter' because it works for me!

My "right now" decision was to go to the gym and not make mistakes with my fork that I could not repair at the gym. It was time to actually make a sane and sober decision and stick to it. In order to RESET, you have to choose something you can do

NOW to start the process. 'Someday' is too far away. You need a 'right now' action to help move you in the right direction.

*"And after you have suffered a little while,*
*the God of all grace, who has called you to his*
*eternal glory in Christ, will himself restore,*
*confirm, strengthen, and establish you."*
—1 Peter 5:10 ESV

RESET is not a rescue it's a resolution! It is being awakened from sleep walking through your own life, deciding that recovery—whatever it is from such as being an alcoholic, overweight, a gambler, stuck in toxic relationships, etc.—is necessary. RESET is a realization that change must happen. At last you are so tired of the negative things in your life hindering your growth and cutting you off from love that you will finally do what it takes and intentionally enter your recovery period.

# We All Struggle

We all need to work on things at different times in our lives, but when the stuff you are working on starts working on you, it is time for a change. Imagine that your life is a box and it starts out empty. You must put in lots of things with love before you can take anything out. You must tend it, sow in to it, nurture it, feed it and love it. Doing things without love is a useless dance and a waste of energy. Doing things with love makes the heart sing and dance! Be accountable! Accountability and Success are friends! You need them both to win at RESET!

Accountability & Success are Friends

Accountability    Success

You can't have one without the other!

# Favor Follows Obedience

*"And all these blessings shall come upon you and overtake you, if you obey the voice of the Lord Your God."*

—Deuteronomy 28:2 ESV

Favor truly does chase obedience. When you walk in wisdom and make wise choices, then you reap a harvest of good outcomes. This is never more clear than when we are walking through a bitter harvest of bad decisions and in need of a RESET. When you are trying to RESET you must be careful who is around you, be careful of significant people

in your life who do or do not support your goals. Push towards the people who have a positive influence and who definitely want to see you flourish. Do not enable negativity or any form of it surrounding you. One of most positive and powerful things you can do is to shield yourself from negativity and more so be very careful who you get counsel from. Create healthy boundaries (or boundaries period) until you have created a strong shield to forge back into that territory safely. This is a war and you need to win! Your life is at stake. Recovery is a process, so keep yourself as safe as possible in the process.

Use caution when talking about your decision to RESET and your plan for working through the process. Getting the wrong advice in this season could be a mistake that lasts a lifetime. I try and really think about who I am getting advice from. I have noticed when getting relationship advice, my married friends give me wildly different advice than my single friends. This is something to consider and weigh heavily on, at least it was for me. Life may not perfect, but it should be happy, or at least happy most of the time. Pay attention to the state of that persons well being who is giving you advice!

"*You will not be afraid of ... the arrows that fly by day.*"
Psalm 91:5

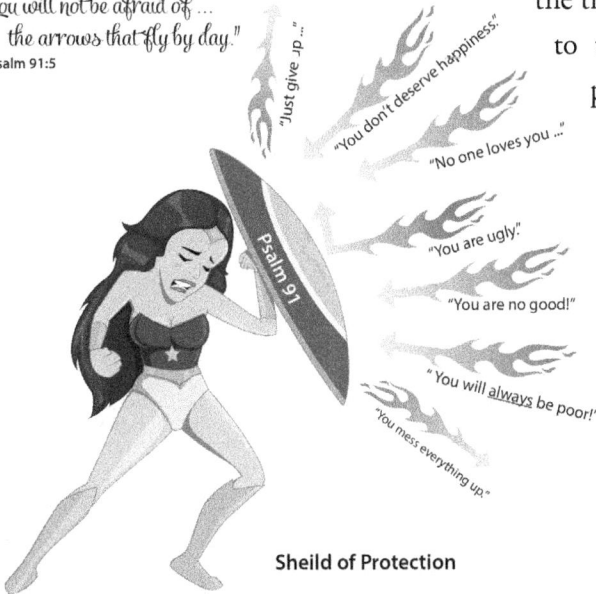

"Just give up..."

"You don't deserve happiness."

"No one loves you ..."

Psalm 91

"You are ugly."

"You are no good!"

"You will *always* be poor!"

"You mess everything up."

**Sheild of Protection**

If I could give you *one thing* in life I would give you the ability to *see yourself* through *my eyes!*

Jacqui & Bello

I ask you to try to do that for yourself. Even if it is just one thing you are great at, please consider the value in you that you hold and respect that about yourself!

*RESET is a call to prepare, a call to be aware,*
*and a call to commit to better life growth.*

—JJ

# You Can Do This!

Now that you are getting ready to take action and we are going to dive into the first RESET please keep in mind that a real RESET cannot be done if you are not willing to give up the fun and do the very hard work. I made serious and painful sacrifices, but I truly felt that it was a life and death situation. It was like my present life was staring down a

barrel of a shotgun and I knew if I did not make the appropriate changes my life was literally shot. All I had to look forward to was a dark, sad, miserable, and broken life! Incremental changes daily repeated become healthy habits. So start by telling yourself, "I love you," every day. Take a walk with your dog … heck … get a dog! Walk up your stairs five times a day. Eat something healthy like salad or fruit. Make a call to someone you love to get a little motivation. Read one thing positive daily. Arm yourself with positive thoughts. Listen to an educational or spiritual book in the car. Do something to start and your RESET will truly gain its own momentum.

Please think about this for a moment. Do your relationships leave you fulfilled and empowered or drained? Seek counsel and mentors in people at the top of their game to create a successful way out in order to get the encouragement and wisdom you need in this process. I often wonder if I had the courage to just stop and leave it all long ago, would I have children now? Would I be married and have true love? Would I be a career woman like I am now really going for it? I want this book to speak to those who are stuck. Maybe you are stuck in love with someone toxic, maybe you are stuck in an unfulfilled dream, or stuck in a bad reality. Get unstuck please. Wake up!

Listen to your own heart. Listen to that lion roaring inside of you and answer the call. Listen to God and have the courage to dream to take just one step … even if just one!

Looking back, my first step was really amazing. There were so many things out of control in my life at that time, grabbing just one thread and holding on tightly enough not to fall apart was a miracle. My first step was to get my body back. It didn't happen overnight and it wasn't easy. In fact, I still work hard on this area, but it was a great place to begin my RESET. Now I will take you on that journey!

## Endnotes

1.  *Breaking the Cycles: Changing the Conversations.* Lisa Frederiksen. http://www. breakingthecycles.com/blog/2013/02/20/understand-brain-maps-change-habit-change-your-life/ Retrieved on 7/5/16.

2.  www.drleaf.com/about/scientific-faqs/ Retrieved on 7/5/16.

# Elements of Truth
# Thermometers

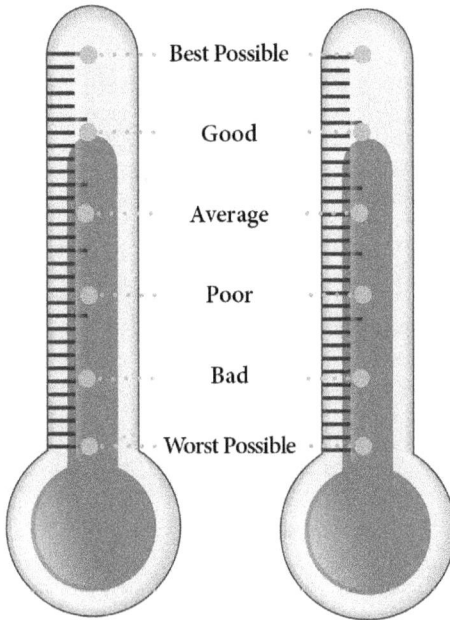

Best Possible

Good

Average

Poor

Bad

Worst Possible

**Where I Am Now**    **Where I Want To Be**

Each RESET category will begin with a thermometer to help you measure your elements of truth—where you are now and where you would like to find yourself on the other side of your RESET.

Being completely honest about your present state and your future goals is key to a successful RESET. Take time to reflect and assess each category. Feel free to share this exercise with others whom you feel will benefit.

*"Be Present, Be Mindful,
Take Action and You Will Win!"*

—JJ

*Chapter Four*

# RESET—
# Health and Fitness

*"Our problems start in our minds and move to our spirits—that's where they fester. So spiritual weight loss is the true (and lasting) RESET."*

—JJ

*"Don't you know that you yourselves are God's temple and that God's Spirit lives in you?"*

1 Corinthians 3:16

I n both life and love we can get emotionally fat. The weight starts layering on as we carry around unprocessed toxic feelings, hold on to unkind words spoken over us and inconsiderate actions that have hurt us. This is why we need spiritual weight loss. Spiritual weight loss is the real solution to the change you need and the empowerment required to have a successful RESET of your health and body. You are a spirit ("pneuma"), you have a soul ("psyche"), and you live in a body ("soma"). Your body is a temple, where your spirit and your soul are housed. When you RESET and become

your healthy self, your outsides and insides can begin to match and live in harmony with one another!

> *"Let food be thy medicine and medicine be thy food."*
> —Hippocrates

## Health & Fitness Thermometer
### Figure 4.1

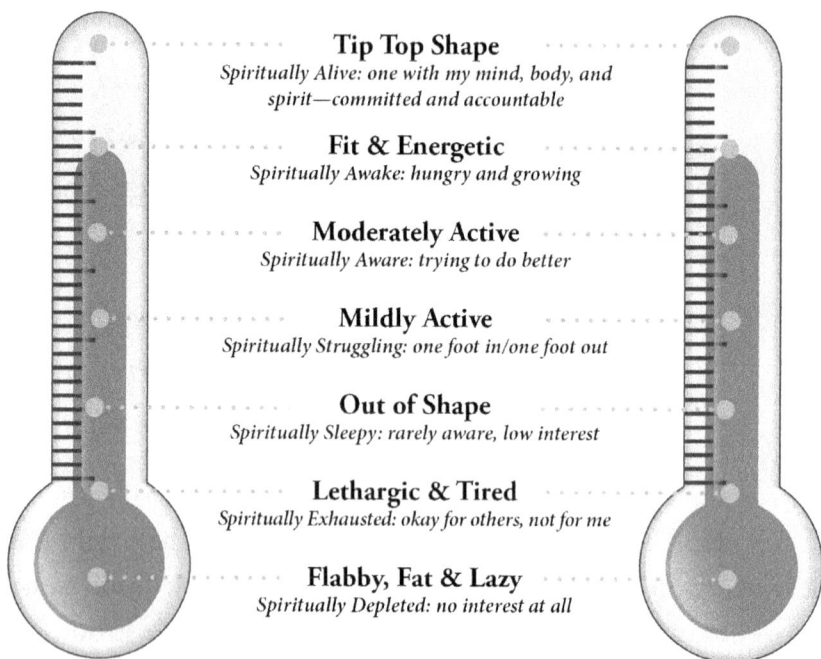

**Tip Top Shape**
*Spiritually Alive: one with my mind, body, and spirit—committed and accountable*

**Fit & Energetic**
*Spiritually Awake: hungry and growing*

**Moderately Active**
*Spiritually Aware: trying to do better*

**Mildly Active**
*Spiritually Struggling: one foot in/one foot out*

**Out of Shape**
*Spiritually Sleepy: rarely aware, low interest*

**Lethargic & Tired**
*Spiritually Exhausted: okay for others, not for me*

**Flabby, Fat & Lazy**
*Spiritually Depleted: no interest at all*

**Where I Am Now**                    **Where I Want To Be**

On the "Where I Am Now" thermometer, mark the category which best fits you in your present health & fitness state. This helps you prepare for your RESET.

Now take a look at the "Where I Want to Be" thermometer and consider where you would like to find yourself in the future. Mark this is also so you can begin to chart your course to reach this important goal!

# Questions for Health and Fitness:

- ❧ Do I feel fat or too skinny?

- ❧ Do I have the energy and vitality to work out and accomplish my goals?

- ❧ Are my sleep patterns affected by my health?

- ❧ Do I give my body clean or dirty fuel? Am I conscious of my nutrition?

- ❧ What choices could I make today that would lead to a healthier life tomorrow?

*"Transmit pain into something of use!"*

—JJ

Following my first RESET and all during my second one, I began to say in my head over and over, "I am a champion! I am a champion!" While reading this chapter I really want you to keep this mantra, "I am a champion!" close to your heart. You must learn how to affirm yourself. Affirmations are oh, so important. Affirmations are confirming things that are true, and oh so necessary for us to hear again and again. In times of stress or struggle, knowing how to affirm yourself can help you talk yourself down off the ledge. It is GREAT when others are around to affirm you, but since you can't always program that to happen when you need it most, you must learn how to affirm yourself.

I often said to myself, "I am a champion!" even though more than half of the time I didn't feel like one! I would reach down deep inside that girl, that old athlete, that old fighter and I would say, "I am a champion!

I am a champion! I will not be beat! I will win, I will flourish, bring it on!" Working out would make me cross my threshold into my power. I knew the best thing I could do for myself was to transmit this pain into something of use.

Even if I didn't feel like it, I would repeat my mantra and do it. I knew after I worked out—or sometimes just forced myself out of bed to take a shower—I would feel better by taking one step … yes, just one step forward. That one step was a moment of positivity that would move me through the difficult moments toward my better self! I wouldn't let it beat me. Notice I did not use the word "defeated" because I believe "defeated" sounds permanent "beat" is temporary. Getting beat can spur you on to success. You beat dough to make it rise, we beat our flesh—our limiting beliefs—and press ourselves forward to become better. So in my vocabulary there is no such word as defeat, there is only temporary pain that will flourish to success. When you succeed in your mind, that success will manifest as a physical reality!

*"We are hard pressed on every side, but not crushed; perplexed, but not in despair; persecuted, but not abandoned; struck down, but not destroyed."*

2 Corinthians 4:8-9

*"The difference between a champion and a contender is a champion finishes the race over and over again until they get the desired results. They know and accept deep in their soul that there is never a finish line. Success is ever evolving!"*

—JJ

I encourage you from the bottom of my heart to be the champion you are! She is in there she is just waiting for you to say hello again! Go find a mirror right now. Look her in the eye and say, "Hello, champion!"

*"Behind the smile I was crying. Behind the smile I was dying."*
**J.J.**

On the Set of Valerie Persaud's Show                On the Set of NJ Housewives on Bravo

These photos took a lot of courage for me to share with you. I was ashamed of myself. I knew I could do better and I vowed to myself I would! Ghandi says "You must be the change you wish to see in the world." I knew in order to change my world my only answer was to change myself, so that I did! I knew that if I got my body back, I would get my mind back and it would set off a chain reaction. I also knew

that it would not only be excess pounds that would fall off, but that weight would also be people. At the time I just didn't realize how many. Clearly from these pictures you can see a whole lot of problems were going on and had been going on for way too long. My physical body manifested all that was internally. My outsides matched my insides— and they were both a hot mess! I was what I ingested and I was what I thought. My lion had roared and now all the dysfunction and unhappy needed to stop.

> *"Don't fall asleep on your life! Wake up and let your spirit flow!"*
>
> —JJ

It was a cold November day when I heard that lion roar. All I can say is my spirit was screaming like it was trapped, my soul like it was literally being smothered. It was saying, no shouting, "Wake up and let me the heck out of here!" I knew it was begging me to wake up and thank God I did!

Later that same morning an email came with a Groupon for a kickboxing bootcamp. My first thought was, "I really could kick something … this sounds like a great idea!" so I texted my friend. She replied, "Come to my bootcamp its up the street. It will change your life!" The roar had worked. It woke me from my slumber and forced me to fight for my life.

I mentioned going to bootcamp in chapter one, and it reminded me of the movie *Sleeping With The Enemy*. Julia Roberts' character learns how to swim so she can escape her abusive husband. She was waiting for her moment to literally jump ship and swim to shore. I would say I was doing the exact same thing. I needed to teach myself how to walk all over again. I had once been a fit, healthy, athletic, confident

woman, but somehow I lost all my healthy habits. Through years of bad relationships and ignoring what was good for me, I had replaced the healthy habits with toxic ones which stole my identity and remade me into an overweight, unhappy, depressed, lethargic, faint copy of the woman I had once been.

You see I realized God designs us all so uniquely. My uniqueness was that I had a long, lean, strong body naturally but it was enhanced because of my dedication to health and athleticism. I had completely lost that part of myself. All of it! I had closed that door by letting life get in the way and putting everything and everyone else first. I forgot who I was. I sure the heck did not know who I was in Christ—I mean how could I as I didn't even know or recognize myself? I became a shell of who I was. I was lost. I was sick spiritually, and I was gonna die if I didn't make an effort and act. Maybe my heart was still beating, but my spirit was dying and once that starts, it continues to manifest physically which was abundantly clear by the enormous weight gain. I believe our bodies try to protect us with

Is your mind and body connected?

... or disconnected?

weight gain or weight loss, or migraines or hair loss, etc. ... as an obvious way to say, "Hey, look in the mirror! I am so trying to tell you something. Please do something about this because I really feel like crap! Can you please help me?"

Bootcamp was a facility where you basically get group personal training. It provided individual attention even though it was a group environment. This was great because I needed a babysitter, but it was also horrifying because I knew the guys who owned it as they came to my spa to get pro tans for their bodybuilding competitions. It was also a nightmare because I would have to face someone who was helping me and realize how out of shape I really was. In this moment I was barely being able to do a push up when many moons ago I could bench at least 140 pounds! Well, let's just say I felt like I was trying to speak a foreign language I had learned long ago, but now couldn't get the words out because my body simply could not perform. I had to face the truth about myself and it wasn't pretty. In that moment I had to choose. I said to myself, "Okay this totally stinks. Am I going do this or quit? go big or go home?" ... and so I stayed. I went to the gym 3-4 times a week. In 8 months I lost 40 pounds. I had muscles again! I had my sculpted legs back, I was back ... and I was happy, sort of.

I knew I still had a lot to do, but now I at least knew this girl again. I could continue to build my strengths one step at a time. I also had that serious business travesty and debt to deal with. Lets not forget about my relationship situation either. Getting my body back was step one. Achieving step one gave me courage to take steps two, three, and four. I needed to become spiritually strong so I could move forward and embrace all the other RESETs necessary. But I had to start somewhere and this was the mountain I climbed that gave me some perspective. It kept me looking over it all with hope! My physical strength helped me find my spiritual strength again. It would be my asset because I could now think clearly.

# Replace the Stronghold

*For God has not given us a spirit of fear and timidity, but of power, love, and self-discipline.*

2 Timothy 1:7

*"When you don't close the chapters you keep reading the same book."*

—JJ

A stronghold of the mind can be described as arguments, philosophies, reasonings, or schemes. When you rid yourself of a negative, limiting stronghold you MUST replace that ideology with a positive belief that cancels its power over you.

If you rid yourself of a stronghold, such as fear, you must replace it with a new one, such as love. You must completely fill the void left in your mind when fear leaves, or something equally as evil and debilitating will take up residence in your mind and continue to do you harm.

Now because I did not say goodbye to all the cousins in the Stronghold family and invite a new healthier family to take their place, a second RESET was needed for me just a few years later. No, I am not kidding. RESET happened again! This time at least I knew what to do because I had the tools, but my heart was broken. I was devastated. The lies and deceit from my ex and my Mother were bitter blows and I was angry. They told me they had my best interests at heart, but a lie, is a lie, is a lie and my spirit was damaged. My spirit was so sad!

Now more than ever before I needed spiritual weight loss. I learned that the truth had been kept from me for 3 1/2 years. I had just

discovered that my boyfriend was having serious financial problems and had been borrowing money from my mother all this time. She had been lending him money she did not have (she is retired) and never told me. I thought to myself, *She is <u>never</u> recover from this, how will she <u>ever</u> get this money back? ... She is retired! How did this happen?* The burden of discovery was so heavy.

I thought we were getting engaged. In fact, he had gone with my mom to pick out a ring and put money down on it—only to return and get his money back. My spirit struggled to carry the load. During this season, my dear friend took me to hot yoga. It was so hard I thought I was going to pass out, but I didn't. I was unexpectedly surprised! I loved the spiritual aspect of this practice. It seemed that every time I went, my instructor (who is now my best friend and definite soul sister) would say something profound and it would resonate deep within me. I would almost cry and sometimes I did without being obvious. It was so darn hot in there, no one would know they were tears, it could have been sweat! Regardless, I needed this kind of bodywork for my soul. Yoga changed my life. I have learned how to meditate as well which also changed my life. I think I had the wrong idea of yoga and meditation as I thought this was a more Eastern Practice. I thought I would not have anything in common being of Christian faith, and then I realized God is inside of me and I can pray to God and Jesus the entire time I was in yoga and meditation.

Yoga has become an important practice for me, and I do it in a way that honors God and honors me. It is about self love and there is no more love than that which is from God, so it just clicked and I have a balance and clarity that I have never had in my life before. I have truly learned how to be a conduit to the Holy Spirit and my faith has grown even more. I have learned how to be in touch with and listen to my body in ways I never did before. I knew that it was official I was RESET yet again, only this time—better and stronger.

When I modeled I was so mean to myself. I did everything wrong. The lies that our youth shows, that young exterior facade doesn't allow us to see what we are really doing to ourselves internally. My insides and outsides definitely did not match. This picture tells it all.

*"In the darkest time of my life is when I found the most faith."*
J.J.

*"I was ashamed. I knew I could do better ... and I did!"*
J.J.

As a young lady in my 20s and as a model I was thin, in shape, and I looked happy. I was not! I was starved, obsessed, hated myself—mostly because I was so critical of my body. I would drop 10 pounds constantly even though I didn't need too, doing all the wrong things such as crazy diets, diet pills, laxatives, and definitely a little puking when necessary. This picture is full of lies.

The middle picture … well, I think we know that story, and this last picture is me now, all these years later. This girl I like. This girl I finally love. This girl is strong inside and outside. This girl puts God first, is healthy, in shape, doesn't smoke, doesn't drink excessively, runs in races, helps and loves her family and friends, but most of all, takes the time for herself to sow into self love and fitness in all the ways that are important in order to live in vitality and joy! This girl I will keep. She is who God designed me to be. She is the result of my real RESET! I am finally walking in my truth. No lies with this girl: what you see is what you get!

> *"Declare the past, diagnose the present, foretell the future."*
> —Hippocrates

We all go through different forms of RESETs. I had two big ones: the ending of businesses, and the ending of relationships. To know someone doesn't love you (or really love themselves enough to do the things they should or promise to do) can effect many areas of your health. It is hard to know someone doesn't love you the same way you love them, or think about you the way they used to, or maybe they simply do not love you at all. The obvious pulling away between two people is something that is real and can be felt. Whether we want to admit it or not, there is an undeniable truth about it. It may not be spoken about out of pride or embarrassment, but it is real and it takes a toll on your emotions big time! Which, in turn, translates to your health and more importantly to your spirit. Emotions are your guidance system. They can tell you the current state of your life and relationships. Feeling the change in the relationship is as obvious as feeling the temperature changing in a room from hot to cool. You feel the cool breeze sweep through, and

often you're not sure of the reasons why, you just know it in your heart to be true even if you wish it were not.

A relationship which once felt like warm sunshine has become chilling darkness. You can't help but wonder why? This affects your mind and therefore your health. It completely destroys your motivation to work out and be healthy—it doesn't seem to matter.

> *"Sometimes you have to give up*
> *everything to get everything."*
>
> —JJ

When you are processing such pain, your spirit is heavy, your soul is sad. This is a dangerous time for your body because sadness affects your physical well being. This is when you have to find strength within and do something positive. Even if it is as simple as taking a walk outside, do it! This will help you to surrender and let go of the pain.

Sometimes you have to give up everything to get everything. Giving up everything allows you to start with a clean slate. That "everything" is defined as all that no longer serves you! This includes unhealthy eating, drinking, drugging (stop this madness if you are), smoking, and most importantly negative thoughts. Create a new story for yourself. Your focus determines your reality. What you focus on, you become. So sometimes when we focus on what we DON'T want, or who we DON'T want to be, that's exactly what we become. Now instead of focusing on what you don't want for your life, focus instead on what you DO want. Focus on the I AM truth that you want to and can walk in.

My focus is that I AM love, I AM encouragement, I AM strong physically and mentally, I AM inspired as I aspire to help others! I AM a lighthouse of love. I have a heart that I want to share with the world!

This is what I emit from myself. Staying healthy and fit allows me to practice my I AMs. It lets me live and walk in my truth. It keeps me centered and grounded. What is your I AM and how can you manifest it physically and practice it daily?

In order to really start the physical and health RESET, you must achieve spiritual weight loss first by peeling off the layers of truth. You must take yourself back. Yes this will be painful, but it is necessary.

*Layers added over the years result in heaviness.*

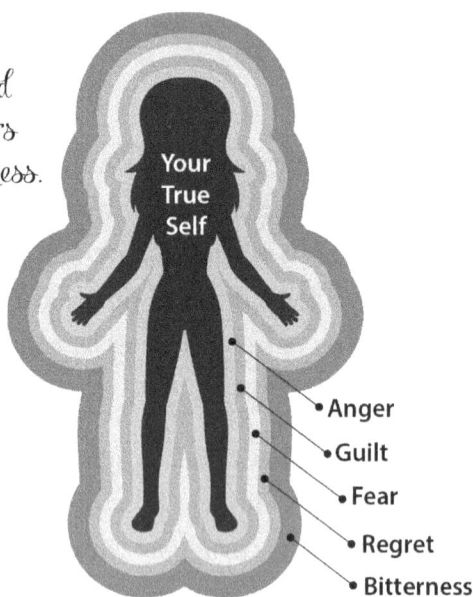

Your True Self

• Anger
• Guilt
• Fear
• Regret
• Bitterness

*Spiritual weight loss will remove these layers and reveal the True Healthy You inside!*

Think back to when you first started having discord with your body, your health, and your spirit. When did you start bullying yourself and talking negatively to yourself and why? Did someone do this to

you first and did it start the process? Did someone teach you not to love yourself and your body? When did you start this negative inner dialogue with yourself?

I remember when mine began. The first was when I was younger. My parents divorce caused me a lot of pain and chaos. They were all over the place. There is no denying their absolute love for me and yes they tried and did their best, but they did not love themselves so they could not offer healthy love to me in those years. By the time I was eight years old, I felt like I was parenting them—I kid you not! I was too young to take care of my own needs, let alone handle the needs of broken people looking to me for strength. My confusion, anguish, and frustration manifested into me abusing my body. It was a cry for help. No help came.

This was the beginning, the planting of bad seeds of this bad relationship I would have with myself mentally and physically. My parents' situation annoyed me, I wanted normalcy, I wanted no more dysfunction. The plight of focusing on what I didn't want most resulted into what I had most. There I was, the starring role in a self-fulfilling prophecy of dysfunction and disaster.

I was a total mess inside, though on the outside no one knew because I was young and looked healthy. In our youth, our bodies can deal with all kinds of torture for a long time before it shows, but on the inside I was broken and defeated. I lived angry and in fear. I lived disappointed and covered this hurt with destructive thoughts and harmful habits.

Because of this I was not living up to my potential and I definitely was not living in my truth. I was not embracing all the gifts God gave me and therefore I was delaying my purpose. If only I knew then what I know now, I could have saved myself a ton of heartbreak!

Regardless of it all I was lucky, my body seemed resilient … until it wasn't. Overall I tried to love my body to the best of my ability until somebody told me I shouldn't. I remember this day like yesterday as I went to see my little cousins at the beach and my ex told me that I didn't look good in my bikini. This was when I first learned body shame. I never had body shame before that moment, and I realize now that is when my next real weight struggle started. Like all things, it started in my mind first and then when stress kicked in and grew, the internal issues turned external. For years and years and years I lived this way. Feeling up and down and letting my outsides and insides match in a negative way and sometimes not matching at all.

When people put you down enough you start to believe it and if you allow it, you start to become it—which I did. Even though the first time I was on the beach with my cousins I did look good in my bikini, by the next time I was with my cousins in a bikini, I didn't. I became what I was told I was. Passive aggressive behavior can do that. It sucks you in. One minute someone tells you that you are beautiful, then the next they are putting you down. It is a form of control whether we realize it or not, it is. It is also a way people envelop you with their low self esteem. I know you are wondering why I allowed it. Why did I stay with someone who put me down? The truth was I was the queen of tolerance. I also liked the companionship and I loved this person. For years it was more good than bad. He put me down often, but he also put me on a pedestal too. There was just enough good to make me tolerate the bad. Nothing was constant in those years, it was unbalanced. I was very young and I truly didn't know better. Like the great Maya Angelou says, "When

*When people put you down enough you start to believe it … you start to become it*

you know better you do better." Now I know so now I do. It's really that simple!

Body shame is horrible. Shame on me and shame on you for having it! You should love all of you every moment of the day. Please try, I mean really try. It may seem silly, but in order to encourage positive change within yourself, you need to hear yourself say nice things out loud about your body. Your cells hear positive and negative language. We are mostly water (see the study by Masaru Emoto on pg. 95) and our cells are affected by our thoughts because they generate feelings and truth. Our thoughts manifest into the physical reality. Your brain and body believe what you tell them, so tell them something positive. Please learn to tell yourself something positive daily, even if you only say one nice thing to yourself all day. Reward your body by using it and making it feel good by exercise. In this illustration it briefly describes the rewards of the different forms of exercise and how it will positively impact your life. There are so many choices out there to work out. There is truly something for everyone, so it's up to you to choose what you're attracted to that you will enjoy. If you enjoy the activity, you will look forward to making the effort to do it!

## PHYSICAL EXERCISE

It goes without saying that physical activity is important for maintaining your health. It is critical at every age. Government recommendations include that children and adolescents (6-17 years old) get at least 60 or more minutes of moderate-to-vigorous intensity aerobic physical activity. The recommendations continue that children and adolescents require muscle- and bone-strengthening activities at least three days each week.[1]

The report goes on to say that adults (18-64 years old) should get at least two and a half hours (150 minutes) of moderate-intensity aerobic physical activity each week, coupled with strengthening activities (like push-ups, sit-ups, and lifting weights) at least two days each week.[2]

There are so many ways to exercise! It doesn't have to mean that you join a gym, buy stylish fitness gear, and hire a personal trainer! Start wherever you are even if its just fifteen minutes a day. Be consistent and dedicate time to it every week. Below is a list of just a few ideas that can get you moving and start improving your health and fitness:

- Bike riding
- Canoeing
- Ballroom (or other) Dancing
- Gardening
- Walking Briskly
- Water Aerobics
- Running the Vacuum Cleaner
- Playing with Children at a Park (pushing them on swings)
- Swimming
- Jumping On A Mini Trampoline

For more vigorous exercise try things like:

- Jumping Rope
- Running or Jogging

- Playing Basketball, Soccer, Tennis, or Racquetball

- Bicycling on Hills

- Swimming Laps

- Martial Arts

- Mowing the Lawn (push mower)

The important thing is to do **something**! Just get moving and in time move more. Aerobic activities will make you breathe harder and increase your heart rate. You'll know if it is moderate aerobic activity because you can talk while doing it, but you can't sing. If your activity is vigorous, you will only be able to say a few words without stopping to catch your breath.

Combined with this, be sure to do activities that strengthen your muscles, activities that strengthen your bones, and activities that involve stretching and balance. All these will help you be stronger, more flexible, and more stable—not just body, but mind and soul as well.

## YOGA

Millions of adults practice yoga. Most do it do maintain their health and well-being, but others do it to treat specific medical conditions or for musculoskeletal conditions. Many people practice yoga to relieve low-back pain and also report it helps with depression.[3]

My own personal journey has introduce me to yoga. Yoga coupled with meditation and prayer have been a powerful key to keeping my body, mind, spirit, and soul fit and healthy.

## MEDITATION/PRAYER

I have found meditation decreases my stress and helps me focus my thoughts on positive things. It quiets my mind and allows my creativity to flourish. Studies show my experience is backed up by science and the benefits don't stop there, other health benefits such as improved immunity, lower inflammation, and decreased pain have also been documents. Other studies show that meditation sharpens attention and memory as well.[4]

I do it because it makes me happy! How? Meditation has been shown to increase positive emotions while decreasing anxiety, stress, and even depression. Meditation can increase your social connection and improve your emotional intelligence as well. The natural progression is an increase in compassion and feeling less lonely.[5]

Because I enjoy meditation so much, I was really excited to learn that it actually changes my brain! Studies show it increases grey matter as well as increases volume in areas of the brain related to emotion and self-control. Even cortical thickness increases which is the part of the brain related to paying attention.[6] Wow!

> *"The quality of our life depends on the quality of our mind."*
>
> —Sri Sri Ravi Shankar

Whatever your reasons, know that practicing meditation is a healthy habit that improves the quality of your life.

## NUTRITION

Nutrition is a topic we can talk about forever, and like exercise it is completely and solely a personal choice and discovery. What worked for me may not work for you. I encourage you to really dedicate some time learning what works for your body and what doesn't. Your body is a machine and it needs the proper fuel to run. Your body is also a temple. Treat it like such because the more you love your body the more it will love you back by feeling good and performing the way you want it to. That also means looking good people!

*We are what we eat. Which one are you?*

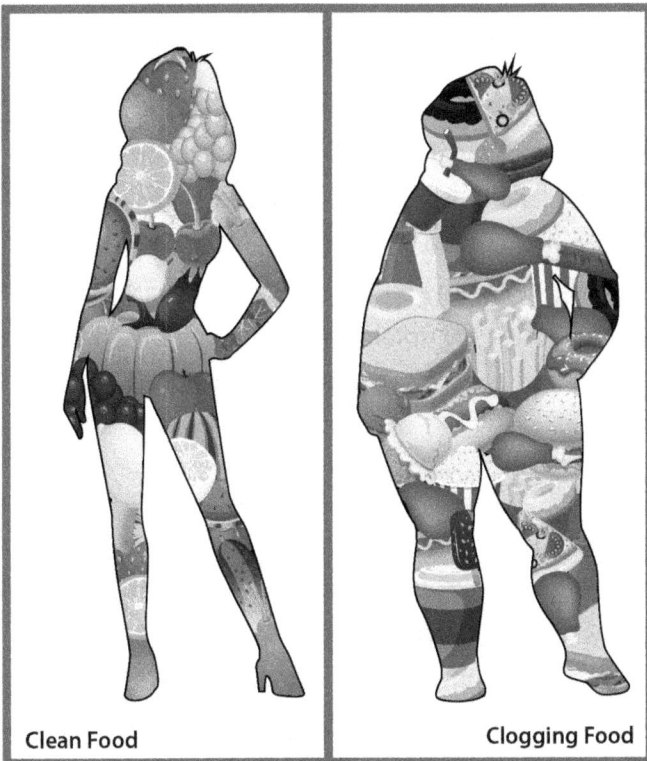

Clean Food                    Clogging Food

> *"Do you not know that your bodies are temples*
> *of the Holy Spirit, who is in you, whom you have*
> *received from God? You are not your own."*
>
> 1 Corinthians 6:19

Personally I follow these guidelines:

- I eat clean, meaning not many processed foods.

- I do not eat white foods or much sugar (only on occasion).

- I eat a lot of protein and vegetables.

- I drink black coffee.

- I drink a ton of water (and I am truly in love with seltzer water).

My friend, Dr. Joe Colella, gave me the best nutritional advice I have ever gotten… and I actually listened. Guess what? It actually worked! Dr. Colella is a bariatric surgeon who has dedicated his life to helping people fight obesity. He wrote *The Appetite Solution*[7] and I suggest reading it. Dr. Joe told me to decide what I wanted to weigh and eat that amount of protein (number of grams) a day. So, if you want to weigh 100 pounds, then you eat 100 grams of protein a day. It's that simple!

He said to me, "Jacqui, I know this is hard to eat that much food, but I suggest supplementing your intake with whey protein and make sure it is low sugar." One of the many suggestions he offered was eating foods by Quest, high protein amounts, and low sugar. I absolutely love and can not live without them![8] I eat their potato chips, shakes, and bars everyday, literally. This has changed my life and helped me to up

my game. I truly do not struggle anymore and I am lean. It works—I am living proof!

He also says that you cannot fix the mistakes of the fork in the gym.

## *"Love The Problem Away!"*

—JJ

So I say stop ingesting poison, that also includes your thoughts as they are the precursor to your food choices. Hippocrates says this, "Let food be thy medicine and medicine be thy food." Ask yourself is food your medicine or your poison? Please be mindful what you ingest because it creates not only your current mood and current body, but also your future mood and future body.

Your food intake is a direct result of your overall health, so please love yourself! If this is a big problem, then love the problem away by making conscious decisions to better your health and make your engine—your temple—run better, feel clean, pure, and empowered!

Get in harmony with your health. You can feed your body better once it's fed with love. I look back at all those years I did not live this way and in those years my anesthesia was bad thoughts, food, alcohol, and cigarettes. I loved and hated them all equally depending on what day it was. The spirits I was attracted to were fear and anger. That was the vibration I was always on everyday, day in day out, and it showed.

> *Get in harmony with your health and feed your body with love*

Until I separated from that part of myself there was no reprieve. It was almost like I was at war with myself and until I changed my mindset,

it was impossible to win. It is a hamster wheel of hell and your spirit is truly under fire!

I am a product of my thoughts because thoughts trigger and turn into my feelings. I will always be okay. I trust that God will take care of me. I will believe His thoughts about me. I will speak His words over myself. Napoleon Hill says, "Mind your thoughts and keep them positive and if you can get control of that it is the greatest achievement one can make."

Our bodies are the temple of the Holy Spirit.[9] From the food we eat to the liquid we drink to the thoughts we think. If you wouldn't eat an entire cake because you know how bad it is for you, then why on God's green earth would you allow constant chatter about how no one loves you, or that you are fat, or you're never gonna live up to that expectation or standard. We must choose our thoughts as wisely as we choose the food we eat, as the friends we keep. You are a reflection of those you surround yourself with. You are a reflection of those thoughts you surround yourself with also, so choose well or it will effect your entire life.

It's amazing that the answer is this simple, and its solely up to you. Your mind is truly the only thing you have complete control over. Stay prayerful to stay centered and in perspective of what's really important. Your positive thoughts protect your spirit and keep you full of love and inspiration.

We do better when we know better. Now that I know better I must do better. My success is mine to enjoy, my failure is mine to endure. It is entirely up to me to be my best self. Now, I challenge you to be yours!

# *Love the problems away*

Before RESET

After RESET

Let go of your burdens. Give them to God. Be free. Live again!

# *Reset Rituals—Tips To Go*

- Get Moving
- Eat Clean
- Meditate/Pray
- Give Thanks
- Love The Problem Away

## Endnotes

1.  Retrieved from http://www.fitness.gov/be-active/physical-activity-guidelines-for-americans/ on 7/12/16.

2.  Retrieved from http://www.fitness.gov/be-active/physical-activity-guidelines-for-americans/ on 7/12/16.

3.  Retreived from https://nccih.nih.gov/news/multimedia/infographics/yoga/text on 7/12/16.

4.  Retreived from https://www.psychologytoday.com/blog/feeling-it/201309/20-scientific-reasons-start-meditating-today on 7/12/16.

5.  Retreived from https://www.psychologytoday.com/blog/feeling-it/201309/20-scientific-reasons-start-meditating-today on 7/12/16.

6.  Retreived from https://www.psychologytoday.com/blog/feeling-it/201309/20-scientific-reasons-start-meditating-today on 7/12/16

7.  *The Appetite Solution* can be found at: http://theappetitesolutionbook.com/.

8.  You can learn more about Quest products at: http://www.questnutrition.com/.

9.  1 Corinthians 6:19.

## Chapter Five

# RESET—Relationships

*"All the makeup in the world can not
make this right anymore!"*

—JJ

*"People show you who they are, believe them."*

Maya Angelou

Relationships are the heartbeats of our life. There are many different forms of relationships—love, family, friendships is personal and very important. Relationships are all encompassing, they affect our hearts and therefore, our lives. While writing this book I went through two different RESETs. Both were awful, but enlightening. The pain I endured left me worthy to walk in freedom as I found my strength.

We cannot always control our circumstances, but we can control our response to those circumstances. We may not be able to change everything, but there are always things we can (and must) change. It is easier to live with your eyes closed than open. Denial and delusion are loyal friends. They make it easier to live as a victim than to take

responsibility and become a victor. I waited until the pain was great and all joy was gone before I started my first RESET. I hope you will realize the power to change earlier than I did. I hope you will start your RESET right now, or better yet avoid the need to make a RESET and listen to the red flags.

Use the Relationships Thermometer below to help you assess where you are right now and where you would like to be.

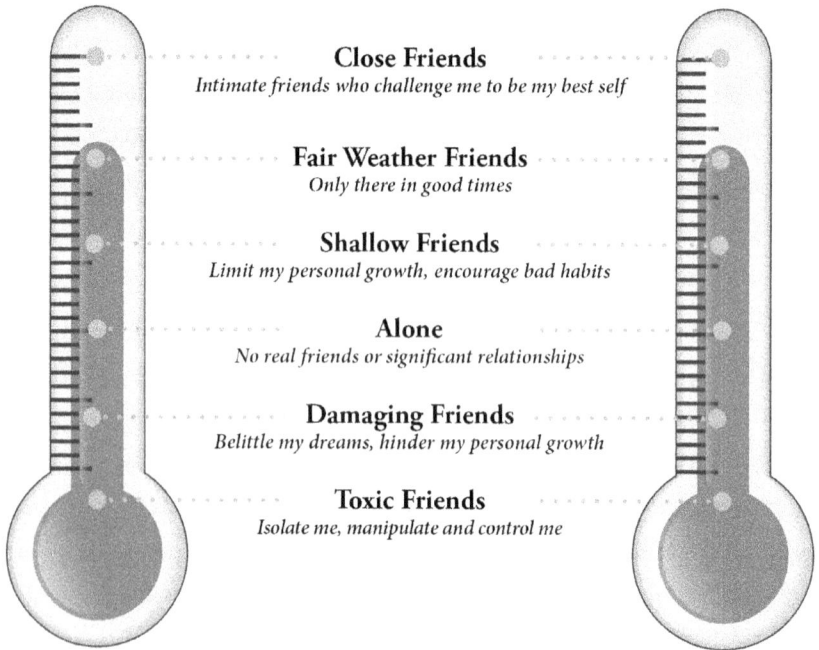

### Relationships Thermometer
#### Figure 5.1

**Close Friends**
*Intimate friends who challenge me to be my best self*

**Fair Weather Friends**
*Only there in good times*

**Shallow Friends**
*Limit my personal growth, encourage bad habits*

**Alone**
*No real friends or significant relationships*

**Damaging Friends**
*Belittle my dreams, hinder my personal growth*

**Toxic Friends**
*Isolate me, manipulate and control me*

**Where I Am Now**                    **Where I Want To Be**

On the "Where I Am Now" thermometer, mark the category which best fits you in your relationships. Even if painful, this assessment is necessary to begin your Relationships RESET.

Now take a look at the "Where I Want to Be" thermometer and consider where you would like to find yourself in the future. Mark this also so you can begin to chart your course to reach this important goal!

Maybe your heart is in the right place—I certainly thought mine was, but unfortunately my brain was out to lunch! Loyalty is a quality I have always valued highly, but any strength stretched out becomes a weakness. I clung to loyalty long after it became obvious that I was loyal to something lethal. It was hard to find the courage to overcome the challenges before me, but I did it. I am proud of myself. I know that whatever is facing you right now, however badly you are in need of a RESET, you too can come out of it victoriously!

## What is Love?

*Love is patient, love is kind. It does not envy, it does not boast, it is not proud. It does not dishonor others, it is not self-seeking, it is not easily angered, it keeps no record of wrongs. Love does not delight in evil but rejoices with the truth. It always protects, always trusts, always hopes, always perseveres. Love never fails.*

1 Corinthians 13:4-8

I believe in the kind of love where you share all your hopes, dreams, and desires with that person—your soul mate—is possible. Isn't that what love is? Sharing your whole self with someone and they share their whole self with you? Isn't true love when someone is your everything? Should love not be a safe place where you can lay all your cards on the table and say, "Hey I love you, all of you, and I might not be perfect but here I am. Please love me forever and I will do the same"?

> *"People are often unreasonable and self centered.*
> *Forgive them anyway. If you are kind, people may*
> *accuse you of ulterior motives. Be kind anyway."*
>
> Mother Teresa

We all just want to be loved. Love is the stamp on our hearts and souls. Love is the imprint we are left with. It breathes in and out of us and fuels our emotions. It is the GPS guidance system of the heart and when left unattended, it suffers greatly with grave results sometimes. But when attended, it blooms like the most magical and beautiful garden in all of heaven!

### Love Window

**Open Window**

Hope
Energy
Joy
Trust
Endless Opportunities

**Closing Window**

Please Listen to Me
Please Talk to Me
Please Show Me Affection
Please Value Me
Please Consider Me

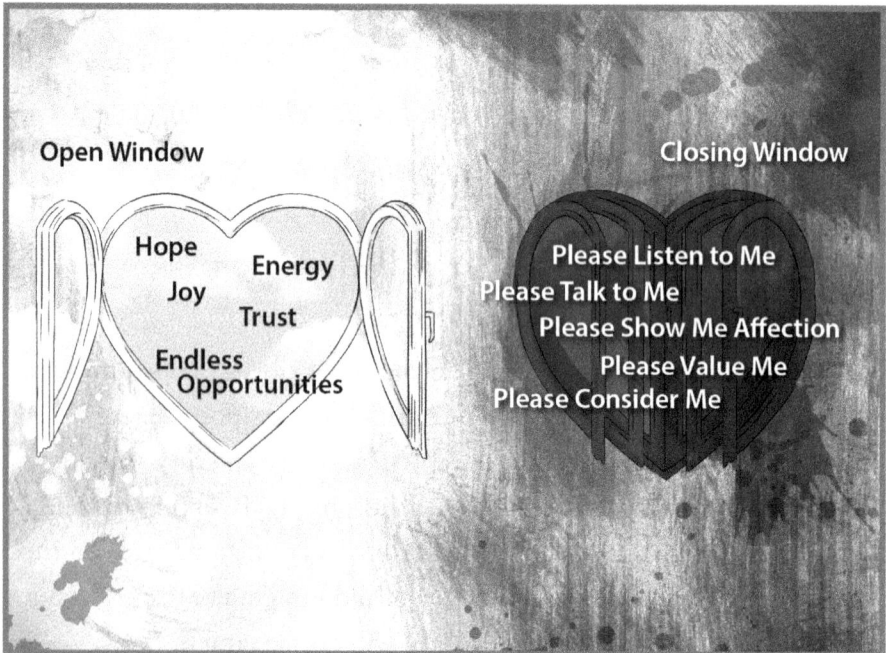

**What is the tone of your relationship?**

# Love Yourself First

Learn to love yourself first. Hope dies hard. You do not have to beat yourself up because of being in or finding yourself in a bad relationship, but once you know it is toxic you do have to take responsibility to get out of it! The key to a beautiful future is in your hands and your hands only! Time is the precursor to truth. You have to be no and do no if you can't say no. Learning to say no is a powerful form of self love. It demonstrates that you honor your identity. Following are some questions to help you assess where you are right now in your key relationships and determine what needs to be RESET.

# Relationship Questions

- What doors are still open in your life that need to be shut?

- Is there anyone in your life that has a darkness about them? Is there someone who causes you to feel low or just emotionally wiped out when you think about them?

- Who or what do you need to say good-bye to in order to truly start your RESET?

- Is there something you have been fighting for that you realize now that it is not going to be? Are you willing to surrender that dream and stop putting energy into something that bears no fruitfulness … will you let go?

- Do your relationships leave you feeling fulfilled, empowered, and energized or downtrodden, depressed, or drained? (For example: Have you ever come home feeling excited about something, but when you share it with the wrong person they

steal the wind from your sails and you feel deflated and dejected rather than happy at the reflection?)

- Are you sick of being someone's afterthought when they are your only thought?

- What is the state of your relationship with you? How can you enjoy your relationship with yourself starting today? How can you help yourself feel more happy, joyful, and fulfilled? (For example: yoga, taking a walk, running, dancing, meditation, prayer, music.)

*"It is the love that we seek in our lives and the loss and pain that we must all suffer that teaches us the most about ourselves. Our true character is revealed in these evanescent moments that are the heartbeat and song strings of our lives. May we all relish in these moments because while fleeting, it is for them that we have grown into our own."*

—JJ

If food is medicine for the body, what is our medicine for the heart and soul? It is love. But what if that love is unbalanced and unhealthy? Does that make it poison, and then does that poisonous love strike us and run through our veins like a venom? Is this why they say love bites?

I would say the world revolves around love. Great ideas are formed with love. Once the seed is planted it is the love for our ambition to bring these great ideas to fruition that makes them grow, but when does the love take a detour? Is it surrounding yourself with the wrong people? They say the five people you surround yourself with are who

you are, and who your life mirrors most. If this is true then why the heck don't we choose wiser? I've been pondering this so much that I thought maybe this is why my life was on such a hold. My bad choices in love were truly sabotaging my life. I needed it to end and now! Hence, my RESET.

- Who are the five people you are surrounded by?

- How can you take the steps to change them if they need changing?

# When Love is not Enough?

So there I was, into my second RESET at this point. I had well over a decade invested into two relationships that started fine but turned toxic. My desire for my own "happily ever after" still remains strong. I know God will send me the right partner in due time. I know I chased after this dream with the wrong men for too long. In the end, I was living from a bad equation: **Complacent + Comfort = Coward.** I was definitely a prime example of this. I was being a coward. Those who are not cowards have courage, they are warriors, heroes, champions, and conquerors. But the journey from coward to courageous is terrifying! How do I become the champion God made me to be? How do I create a new equation and change the circumstance?

I have a pure heart—I always have. I have no ulterior motives with people. I'm not catty or mean, and I genuinely desire everyone to be happy and okay. My love for God and for people has always helped me to "love the problem away." I had been doing this most of my life, I had just never put language to it, had never defined it. This was the key to my new equation: **Love + Pragmatism = Equanimity.**

By learning to listen to my intuition and then instinctively continuing to "love the problem away" I was able to find equanimity.

**Equanimity**: *mental calmness, composure, and evenness of temper, especially in a difficult situation.*

Equanimity was the key! Life is difficult, but by finding our breath, gaining our composure, and learning how to flow through hard moments and rise above them, we find equanimity. That is the gift! That is a wonderful gift to give yourself in order to maintain balance and a healthy life!

I didn't find it on my own, I sought counsel. You can seek counsel to get the advice you need (and deserve) through a therapist, pastor, priest, life coach, and/or trusted friend. I am also a big fan of paying for encouragement in other ways too! Join a great gym, take yoga, tai chi, dance … whatever you can do to shift your balance and make yourself happy! The answers you need are often right under your nose. You already possess what you require to make a shift and embrace change. You might not like it at first, it may seem hard or even unfair—but a whole, healthy, happy life is worth embracing something uncomfortable in order to reach a larger goal.

*"Letting go of the no will birth in us a new dream of the yes."*

—JJ

When we get our hearts broken we are left with the broken pieces. They feel like razor sharp shards of glass, penetrating the heart, wounding and scarring us. Even though the wounds heal it will always be something that happened to us. Even harder than breaking up with a person, is breaking up with a dream. Whether it is a relationship,

a career, or a business you are breaking up with, accepting that you have to say goodbye is the hardest part. Being willing to say good-bye requires faith, but if we show God courage to let go of a dream, He will birth in us a new and better one. Letting go is a fundamental truth—a necessity you must embrace before you can begin your RESET. Letting go is a key to your better and brighter future!

> "*Show me your friends and I will show you your future.*"
> —Napoleon Hill

In order to encourage growth for yourself please consider this: Are you hanging with "The Has/Beens" or "The Present/Futures"? Your answer to this question is important because it will change the trajectory of your life. Let me first explain who they are.

The Has/Beens are dangerous. They are the people, places, and things that pull you back into the place you are trying to leave. The Present/Futures are safe; they are light and abundant and help propel you forward into the place you need to go. They help you grow into your divine purpose—the person you actually are meant to be.

The Has/Beens are residents of your original comfort zone and your brain lights up like a pinball machine because it is so happy. The Has/Beens know that deep, familiar road map of neural pathways. They are so so hard to leave. They are harder to leave than getting a pair of Spanx off! (Trust me, I wear them and its nearly impossible!)

The Present/Futures, however, are your saving grace. They are incredibly polite, so will not hang around unless you can get comfortable with them and believe you deserve them. This neural pathway is a small, untraveled alleyway in which you need to ride down often to get used to the route. Learn this route and become accustomed to this

route. Once you do it will be like riding a bike down a road that you know well. Even though it has lots of potholes, eventually you don't even think about them, you just keep riding around the bumps and keep going forward.

Who are the people you are surrounding yourself with? Are there more Has/Beens in your life or Present/Futures?

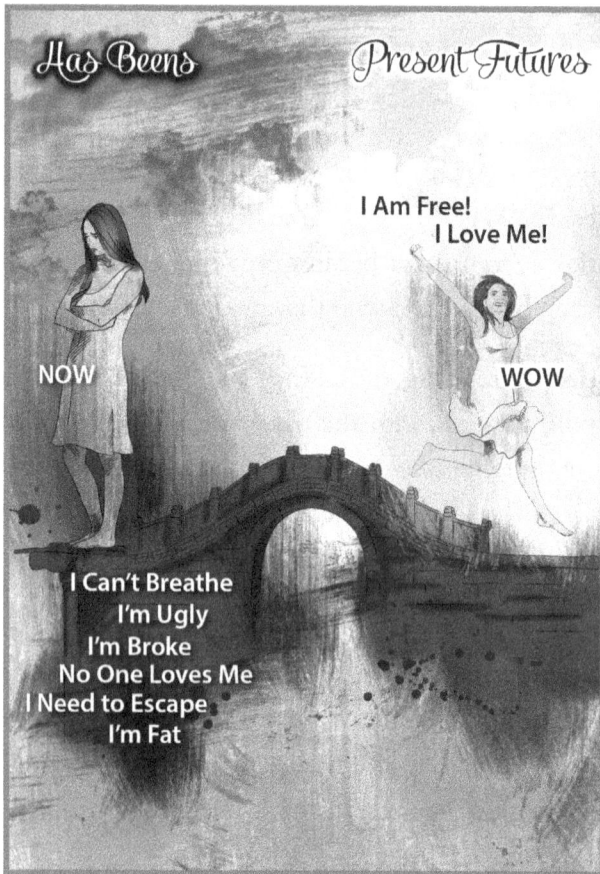

*Has Beens*     *Present Futures*

I Am Free!
I Love Me!

NOW     WOW

I Can't Breathe
I'm Ugly
I'm Broke
No One Loves Me
I Need to Escape
I'm Fat

Imagine you lost 100 pounds. (I imagine between both my RESETS that I lost closer to 400 pounds of physical and emotional weight!) This 100 pounds only signifies the weight of whatever problems you

are facing. Use this analogy to work for you in your own circumstance. Imagine that you have lost this weight—or want to—and you have two dresses of the same exact style and color in front of you, but different sizes. To the left is dress #1: The Has Beens. To the right is dress #2: The Present/Futures. Now they both evoke feeling, great feeling perhaps. One is where you were (or presently are) and the other is where you are going (or want to be).

Now, focus on dress #2. You are in the middle of your RESET and you have 100 pounds to go before that dress will fit. The trick is to do the work and press hard over that bridge ... which is about 10 sizes! Normally, you can figure about 10 pounds per dress size, so the question is this: are you willing to walk with purpose to lose 10 pounds 10 times?

Wow, that seems hard! Well, it is hard. Its painful and it totally sucks, but look how darn pretty that Present/Future dress is and how happy it makes you! Why on God's green earth would you ever want dress #1, the Has/Been dress? I know I don't! This is step one towards experiencing the equanimity you desire!

> *"Above all else guard your heart for*
> *everything you do flows from it."*
> —Proverbs 9:23

I encourage you to guard your hearts and not be fooled by flattery and the things that lead into bad relationships.

One profound question I asked myself while writing this book was, "How can I be an inspiration to others if I can not inspire myself?"

Originally inspired to write the book by my first oh-so-very-traumatic-RESET, I actually endured another before I ever put pen

to paper! Because I didn't say goodbye to the "Stronghold Family" (remember them?), guess who found me? You guessed right! Their cousins, Lack and Co-dependency came knocking and I didn't have enough awareness not to allow them in. But this time their venom hurt more than just me, it hurt people I loved. I was still a little blind, but this time I was also a little bit stronger. Having gone through one RESET made me realize I could do it again. The second RESET was easier because now I had the right tools to use. I was empowered to bounce back more quickly, course correct and get back on the right path faster.

Don't ignore warning signs. Don't make excuses to stay in things that have gone bad … it will ruin your life! Investing your time in the wrong people can be one of the biggest detriments of life. When in love I have learned I want to be in love with someone who first loves God more than they love me! I also want to be in love with someone's present, so they are a present—not in love with their potential which eventually becomes a pitfall! Ask yourself, "Are you capable of allowing someone to love you the way you deserve?" Don't compromise your values and integrity just to be in a relationship.

## Invest in You

People make effort with the things that matter most to them and it shows because there is in fact a big pay off and reward for effort. Take for example, a long beautiful marriage. Well, they will tell you it takes effort … and a lot of it! Let's take another example of a nice well-groomed, attractive appearance. Well, we all know you do not just wake up looking fabulous, so again it takes some effort! So who do you want to invest your time in? Who is worth the effort? Be wise when considering this answer because remember the Present/Future

girl would never attract the Has/Beens friends because their mindsets would never align. So I ask you again: who do you want to invest your time in?

I hope you answered loud and clear, "Me!" Yes, **YOU** are your best investment! You are the only racehorse you should be betting on, because only you can create the outcome you desire. You are worth the investment. You are a sure thing!

"I MAY NOT BE A PRIORITY TO YOU, BUT I AM A PRIORITY TO ME" This should become your mantra. First, that you are your first priority! This leads to asking yourself if you were ever happy in this relationship? I mean really ask, really reflect, and be completely honest with yourself. No excuses. I look back at the previous relationships I had, and I remember many moments of happiness, but they were fleeting. It was always one step forward two steps back. Something would always always happen to take away the joy and darkness would creep in. It became a roller coaster ride. Kind of like always waiting for the ball to drop because chances were it would and did.

# The Love Barometer

How do we rate the oh-so-tipping scales of love? How do we know when its worth it or when its time to say goodbye? The real question is this: **Is your relationship your backup plan?**

Making decisions to meet the needs of others that you know are harmful to you (but you do it anyway despite your better judgment) is dangerous! It is a form of codependency and these are the things that can keep you trapped and stagnant. You can not love someone into loving you more. Either they do or they don't. When someone is unhealthy, you can't make them healthy, no matter how much you love

them. Only they can get themselves healthy again, they have to want it! Loving someone who insists on remaining unhealthy will hurt you.

So, what do I mean by asking if your relationship is your backup plan? Some women and men keep each other around as their backup plan and stay in unhappy relationships for this reason. The backup plan can be staying too long and using it as a roof over your head, or because you do not want to be alone (better to have someone then no one at all), because you need help paying bills, someone to spend the holidays with, a warm body at night, or simply a bad habit you are used too and unwilling to break.

I am guilty of doing this. We all are at times. We all drag things out for the wrong reasons, sometimes we even think they are the right reasons. Sometimes what began as a dream turns into a backup plan and you stay in a stagnant relationship, treading the very murky water because getting out and drying off seems too terrifying. You keep spinning around on that hamster wheel until you finally get off the ride and only then your life can progress. You have been exerting all your energy on spinning that wheel going nowhere. Only after you exit will you have the energy now to actually dream and then birth that new dream. God will send you this dream when you are clear and you can open your heart and spirit to hear it, feel it, and see it!

*As long as you are content to live in your backup plan, you won't risk the adventure of an abundant life.*

As long as you are content to live in your backup plan, you won't risk the adventure of abundant life. You may be blind to the happiness waiting for you because you have settled for miserable and mediocre. Maybe God is giving you a glimpse of that dream right now. Let it give you the

courage to exit the backup plan and enter the plan He has for your highest and best. I did and you can too!

Is it possible that your dream of a relationship is interfering with your actual relationship? In order to move forward, you may first have to break up with that old dream. The old dream has turned into a shackle. God will send you a new dream when your heart is free from the old one. Don't let your heart remain closed off, open up your heart to a new dream today.

Old Dream

New Dream

Failure
Disappointed
Too Busy
Too Tired to Care
Impossible to Achieve
Closed for Business

Inspired
Encouraged
Energized
All Things are Possible
Hearing Clearly
Open for Business

# Questions for Relationships

- Have you alienated people in your life because of your unhealthy relationships?

- Are your relationships with friends and family suffering because of an unhealthy relationship in your life?

- Are you envious of others friends or family relationships and wish yours were like theirs?

- What relationship (or relationships) in your life do you need to cut off, let go of in order to create a healthier you?

- What relationships do you need to mend as a result of your unhealthy relationship?

When you are chartering towards or are in an unhealthy relationship you begin to alienate yourself from your friends and family. It is truly a natural progression that eventually we cut those people off. It can even be your very best friend, siblings, or parents. I found the alienation is attached to the shame and frustration of the failed relationship. We also are ashamed of ourselves because we know deep down that we should be kinder to ourselves and that we could do better. We should be treated better and overall treating ourselves better.

On the other hand, I think we also get tired of hearing about what we need to do. I have learned to be careful of who I share with because sometimes they will only see me in that moment and my essence in their mind will be stuck, so in turn they perceive me as weak. I think some of the people in my life judged me based on the amount of time it takes me to make decisions such as break up, move out, cut the cord if you will. For me, I needed to explore all options to make sure

I was not making a rash decision because I know myself. When I love someone, my heart is like a faucet. I open it completely all the way and the love flows constantly, abundantly and unconditionally. But when I am done, I am done! I always need to make sure once I close the door that I am going to lock it for good!

"You've got to learn to leave the table when love is no longer being served."
Nina Simone

I have now learned that this dragging things out is not totally good though I was like a soul that had passed yet I was lingering, like in the movies. I knew that the death of the relationship had already taken place when the truth of all the lies surfaced. It just took me a lot of time

to break up with the dream, especially because I never saw it coming! I know now how to better read the signs of an unhealthy relationship and how to build a solid one. My second RESET taught me to read the signs more quickly and act before things got out of hand.

# Hurt me with the truth ... Lose me with a lie!

I don't understand why people deliberately hurt others. I don't know why they make decisions they know will hurt someone they love. Choosing to lie is selfish. Choosing to betray another is evil and self-serving. Lying is a coward's way. It never actually works, it just delays pain. Life is so weird in that regard and I am truly not sure why people do what they do when the truth is such a clear path. This in turn is why God makes us create decisions of right and wrong. I have decided when thinking of this not to consider it a crossroad, but a wishbone because that is much more positive. So when life presents you with some very challenging decisions, instead of facing a crossroads, see that you are facing a wishbone to decide which is the happier way!

> "Beware of people who only like you at your worst and not at your best. I have news for you ... They are not your friends."
>
> —JJ

If people do not see you for who you are, and celebrate the greatness in you then find people who do. This led me to realize how important it was to not operate with people who are not on your frequency. We should not lower ours to be on theirs. Some people call this standards, but I am taking this one step further. We are all energy that feeds off of each other, so whatever you feed shall prosper. The Bible tells us so, and I believe it and have seen it with my own eyes.

*"And he shall be like a tree planted by the
rivers of water, that bringeth forth his fruit
in his season; his leaf also shall not wither;
and whatsoever he doeth shall prosper."*

— Psalm 1:3 KJV

So with that being said, if we feed a stagnant situation it will stay stagnant. If we feed a doomed situation it will be doomed. If we feed a hopeful and positive situation, it will catapult into a more hopeful, positive and loving one. So why wouldn't we choose this? When someone shows us who they are, why do we not believe them? Whether it is a boyfriend, boss, friend, or lover, … why do we expect people to change? Why do we think next time it will be different? News flash, it won't. Get over it! Forgive yourself. Forgive them. Move on.

Loy alty + Toler ating = CURED

*To cure a disease, you've got to cut it out of your life!*

*"The avoidance of thyself causes discord in our lives and
it threatens our future. We must face ourselves and create
the reality that we want in order to find true eternal
happiness, which in turn becomes our personal power!"*

—JJ

The choices I make today and everyday reflect my current standard of living and create my future! Napoleon Hill says, "Do not wait for there is never a right time." This leads me to the final things when you are going through your relationship RESET. You are going to experience what I like to call The Lasts and The Firsts!

# The Lasts and The Firsts

The Lasts are how I describe the things you will experience at the beginning of your RESET. The Lasts are the hardest moments, yet they push us out the door to our future selves. Our life can become amazing if we have the courage to trust that this "Last" is necessary and important in order to be our true self and walk in our purpose.

I can remember more Lasts than Firsts. Sometimes our Lasts will surround us for a while. I remember a significant Last: the day my dad walked down the stairs and I knew he did not live with us any more. Another Last was the final day my grandma was alive as it became my first Thanksgiving without her. As I held her hand and prayed with her that morning, she went to heaven. Another Last was the closing breath my grandfather took as I held his hand when he went to heaven. I remember the day I moved out—another Last—because I knew that my relationship was officially over.

The Lasts introduce us to the Firsts. They are the boomerang that gives your life a chance. You get to try yet again! Most times if we have the courage to experience and relish the Lasts then we will really enjoy the Firsts the next time around! Throwing the boomerang can turn the Last of one life into the First of a new one, an exciting and happy one: a first date, a first kiss, a first apartment of your own, a first night out being single, a first Christmas where you are actually

madly in love, a first chance to meet the love of your life because you know you haven't yet!

Have the courage to experience, relish, and really feel the Lasts. Trust and believe it will make the Firsts so much better than you ever imagined … and more! This I know for sure. Breaking up with a dream is scary, but have faith because God will give you a new attainable dream by having the courage to let go of the old one that is not working!

> *"Sometimes you have to give up*
> *everything to get everything."*
> —JJ

# Questions for the Lasts

- What are your Lasts—the profound moments that actually propelled you into the future?

- Do you have any memory of a Last being a moment of regret?

- Do you have any memory of a Last being a fresh, positive abundant start?

- What are some Lasts you need to have to gain the courage to face and put into action in order to live, create, and enjoy the life you desire, deserve, and that God has intended for you. If only you did this … its your leap of faith!

- What will your new First be and what do you look forward to it being once you commit your series of Lasts?

The Firsts are when renewal has started! This is when your healing has really begun and you start to explore your new life. These are big

moments. It could be your first car in your name, the first apartment you decorate all on your own, your first movie alone, your first gym membership, or even your first yoga class. Now you have propelled yourself into your future!

*"Be careful for nothing; but in every thing by prayer and supplication with thanksgiving let your requests be made known unto God."*

—Philippians 4:6

# Questions for the Firsts

- ❧ What are some "A-ha!" moments you can pinpoint which reflect the feeling of moving forward and resonate in you deeply?

- ❧ Do you have a memory or an idea of what a First moment that made you feel empowered?

- ❧ Do you have a memory of a First moment being a new, fresh positive abundant self?

- ❧ What is a First you need to have to gain the courage to face and put into action in order to love, create and enjoy the life you desire, deserve, and what God has intended for you?

Once your series of firsts are committed, map out and draw a picture of your life. Think and pray your life into existence now! Do this daily. It works—trust me I am living proof!

| My Lasts | My Firsts |
| --- | --- |
|  |  |
|  |  |
|  |  |
|  |  |

When your spirit gets sad because of bad relationships, all kinds of other bad things happen. The first step in that is cleaning up your relationships with others and yourself! It is weight loss for your spirit. The spirit is a clear and direct way, direct path, the GPS, and navigation system to pilot us through all our problems. Addressing this takes us straight to the source: where all the problems are stored. Just like a bear stores food for the winter, yet the beauty of it all is this: we have all the answers already inside us. God gifts us with that.

He so loves us and we are of Him, so our souls know the answers we need. Our spirits know. We do have an inner GPS system—it is the Spirit of God alive in you! If it doesn't feel right, it probably isn't right. Learn to trust your inner self. We tend to override these feelings in our spirit and if we learn to follow them and take steps back and access the relationship we can end something before it progresses to a RESET or other consequences. These instincts can prevent heartache. Yet we have a myriad of conversations with ourselves ... we talk and talk and talk ourselves into what we know is wrong for us and out of what we know is right.

I feel like this happens in stages. Its the stages of spiritual anguish and weight gain and the stages of spiritual freedom and weight loss. We will get into this a little more later, but first lets celebrate being victorious by taking the first step to taking the power back in our relationships. Most of all, I encourage you to take the power back in your relationship with yourself. Next lets look at our emotions and build on this to tackle those!

## Chapter Six

# RESET—Emotions

*"Bright lipstick always looks pretty, but
it can also stain your shirt!"*

—JJ

*"Hope is the thing with feathers that perches in the soul—and
sings the tune without the words—and never stops—at all."*

—Emily Dickinson

*A merry heart does good, like medicine,
But a broken spirit dries the bones.*

Proverbs 17:22

## Flip on Your Happiness Switch

Your mind is powerful. It controls your emotions—your thoughts, words, and even your actions. Your mind controls everything! *Everything!* Before we are willing to make a dramatic change, it usually takes pain—sometimes excruciating pain—to project us into the process of healing, of bettering ourselves. I shared my moment when the lion in me roared so loud I had to respond. What causes your pain? What will it take for the lion in you to awaken and roar and push you into change?

Use the Emotions Thermometer below to help you see where you are and assess where you want to be. Once you know you must change, the need to begin will hound you until you decide to do whatever it takes. There is no turning back.

## Emotions Thermometer
### Figure 6.1

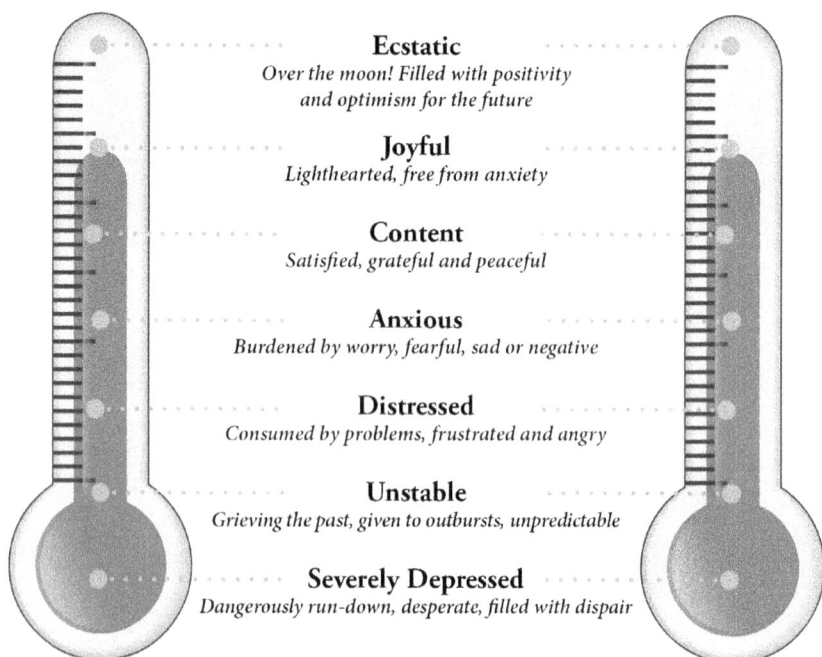

**Ecstatic**
*Over the moon! Filled with positivity and optimism for the future*

**Joyful**
*Lighthearted, free from anxiety*

**Content**
*Satisfied, grateful and peaceful*

**Anxious**
*Burdened by worry, fearful, sad or negative*

**Distressed**
*Consumed by problems, frustrated and angry*

**Unstable**
*Grieving the past, given to outbursts, unpredictable*

**Severely Depressed**
*Dangerously run-down, desperate, filled with dispair*

**Where I Am Now**                                    **Where I Want To Be**

On the "Where I Am Now" thermometer, mark the category which best fits your regular emotional state. This is necessary before you can begin your Emotional RESET.

Now take a look at the "Where I Want to Be" thermometer and consider where you would like to find yourself in the future. Mark this is also so you can begin to chart your course to reach this important goal!

This decision—to do whatever it takes—influenced me greatly. No matter the price, no matter how long it took, I vowed to myself that until I became my best self, I would not focus too much on other personal relationships. Until I could get myself in a place of personal excellence, I was going to be a fierce warrior and do battle with any and everything that kept me down. I know that I am and will always be a work in progress but, I genuinely wanted to be able to say to myself, "I really have my life together! I am doing great!" I knew that when I could say this to myself and mean it, then I would be in position to make the best decisions and be able to trust the decisions I made. I knew personal transformation was going to be a process, perhaps a long process. When I began my second RESET, I found out it is a continuing process—but the process of transformation is highly valuable. If I love myself, then I must commit to becoming (and remaining) my best self.

Part of a successful RESET is learning that it is okay to be happy. You should strive to be happy and start by finding joy in the small things. Happiness starts with a simple smile and a feeling! Happiness is found in using the gifts God gave you. He made me an encourager, and I want to encourage you to celebrate and use your gifts too!

> *We have different gifts, according to the grace given to each of us. If your gift is prophesying, then prophesy in accordance with your faith; if it is serving, then serve; if it is teaching, then teach; if it is to encourage, then give encouragement; if it is giving, then give generously; if it is to lead, do it diligently; if it is to show mercy, do it cheerfully.*

Romans 12:6-8 NIV

I encourage you to love all of you, emotions and all! Move through them, work with them, learn what triggers them, how you express them, and what they mean! Learning to find your why is one of the most important things you can learn. It will change your life forever. Once you learn why you feel a certain way, you will truly be able to move on and really flip on that happiness switch!

# Questions for Emotions

I want you to take an honest inventory of your life! Taking an honest inventory of my life helped me gain control of the outcomes. I was able to write them down and see them for what they were. Here are some questions to help you:

- Do you feel in control of your emotions, or do your emotions control you? Why?

- Are your emotions balanced? Do you feel sad and anxious, angry or depressed more often than you feel happy and content, joyful, or exuberant? Why?

- What stories/ truths do you tell yourself that make you feel happy or sad? Helpless in your circumstances or powerful to change them? When did you first hear these stories and who from?

- Think back to when you were most happy? What were you doing? Who was with you? Why did you feel happy?

- Think back to when you were most sad? What were you doing? Who was with you? What about this made you feel sad?

- Do your outsides match your insides and do your insides match your outsides?

# *Good Vibrations*

Dr. Masaru Emoto studied what our emotions do to us by using water. During the 1990s, Dr. Emoto conducted a series of experiments where he observed the physical effects of words on the crystalline structure of water. They first observed tap water, river water, and lake water. When they froze samples of each, they could get no beautiful crystals from tap water or from rivers or lakes near big cities. Interestingly, where they took water from pristine, undeveloped areas they observed beautiful crystals.

Dr. Emoto and his team next did experiments on water twice distilled from the same company, produced for hospital usage. They froze the water and observed the crystals, then exposed the water to good words, good music, or prayer and observed again.

After the water was exposed to positive vibrations, beautiful crystals would form. Water exposed to negative vibrations would form disfigured crystalline structures. *(The photographs are publsihed as Messages from Water from Hado Kyoiku-Sha.)*[1]

Emoto does not consider his photographs to represent either science or religion, but art. He links it to beauty and how everything on this planet has a deep pursuit of beauty. He believes his photographs demonstrate this truth.[2]

Our bodies are at least 50% water. If Masaru Emoto's observations are correct, then the water that makes up our bodies would respond just as the water in his experiment. Thus, we are deeply affected by our thoughts and feelings. Would the water inside our bodies not reflect that of our thoughts and emotions if water outside our bodies responds to an energy source does? Think about this. Yes, there are a lot

of questions on these findings, but this is something to consider deeply, because your thoughts and feelings are real and they do create your reality. Not a small part of your reality, your whole reality. Therefore, be mindful and considerate of your thoughts as they will be the vibration of your life.

> *"If I don't create the chaos in my life*
> *then I cannot let others chaos effect me. I*
> *must simply breath and let it pass."*
>
> —JJ

# The Anatomy of Your Emotions

After two RESETS, trust was my one big bell ringer! It was going to be my cross to bear, but my choice to bear it and become whole again, or refuse to risk and live bruised forever. It was clear relationships had ruled my life, caused me much trouble. I have experienced all different types. Some have been truly all kinds of amazing, but others have been cancerous, causing disease in my life and making me unhealthy. These bad relationships at times intoxicate me, but leave me unfulfilled and drained. I have now learned to protect myself from people who are negative because their stuff sticks on me. I am now very careful who I let in my personal space because it is not worth losing myself for someone else's selfishness and/or agenda. Boundaries are the key for healthy emotions.

I have created a Toxicology Report of sorts for you. In order to fill this out, you need to be completely honest about what is working and what is not working? What wounds are still oozing, and what has scarred over, but you still bear the mark? What has completely healed?

## *Toxicology Report*

**YOUR NAME HERE**
**PATHOLOGICAL DIAGNOSES (Rank from 1-10 for each):**

SCALE: 10= Fully Alive | 8-9= Healthy | 6-7= Functional
      4-5= Needs Improvement | 2-3= Life Support
      0-1= Dead

_____**HEAD=FINANCES:** Condition of your financial well-being; no anxiety, no fear, preparation, ability to handle emergency

_____**HEART=RELATIONSHIPS:** Condition of your relationship well being; healthy boundaries, mutual respect, personal growth, contentment

_____**SPIRIT=EMOTIONS:** Condition of your emotional well-being; joy, peacefulness, connection with your identity, awareness

_____**LIVER=HEALTH:** Condition of your physical well-being; level of fitness, vitality, strength, endurance, overall health

_____**SKIN=APPEARANCE:** Condition of your physical appearance; comfort with your personal style, attitude concerning appearance

_____**SOUL=FAITH:** Condition of your faith; connection with God, confidence in your purpose, being in right standing

## *Heart Interference*

The heart can cause serious interference in our decisions. When we reach crossroads/wishbones of choice, our hearts sometimes take the lead in the decision—whether right or wrong.

- &#8766; What are the heart barriers which affect your emotions?

- &#8766; What crossroads/ wishbones have you experienced that led you down the wrong path?

- &#8766; What could you have done different?

- What are you glad you didn't choose different?

- When have you gone down the path of least resistance?

- Was it unexpected and forced or planned?

- What did you embrace as a result?

- What path do you need to go down to make your heart whole?

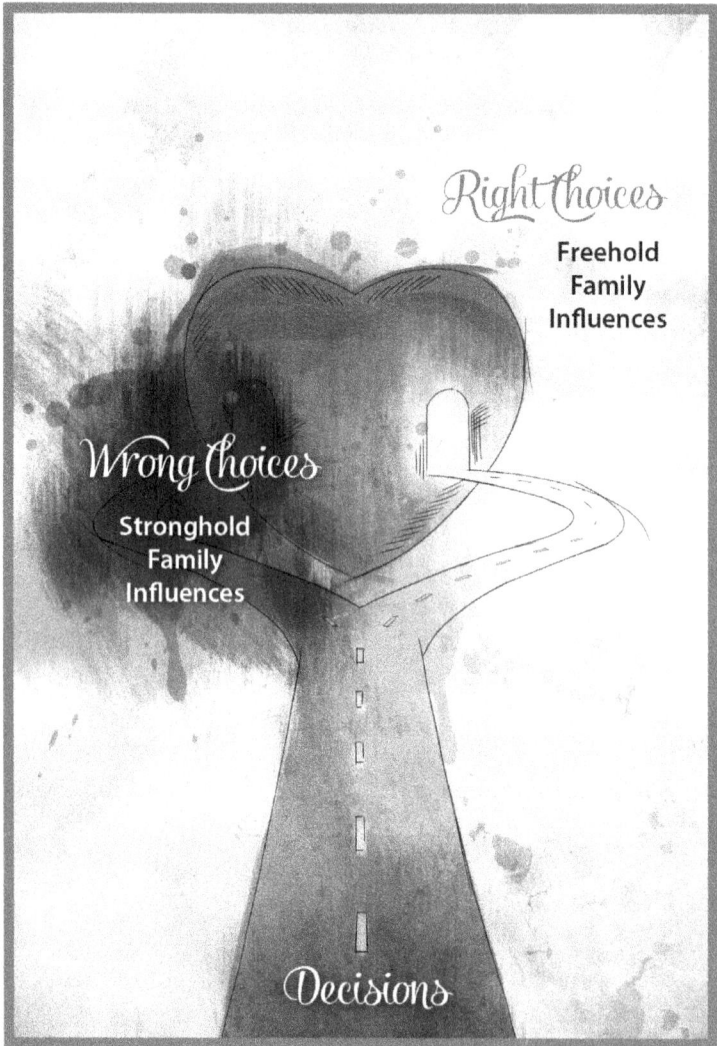

*Right Choices*
**Freehold
Family
Influences**

*Wrong Choices*
**Stronghold
Family
Influences**

*Decisions*

*"You must be awake to love! You must
live with love to be awake!"*

—JJ

Facing your emotions means facing hard truths! The first step to this realizing that needing help is not a weakness and that seeking help is a strength. Only you can help yourself, not your parent, not your husband, wife, sister … no one else can give you what you need. That comes from within first and you need to find it within yourself first. In order to do so, we not only need to acknowledge help is needed, but then we must actually seek it. Help can be in the form of a trusted friend, a therapist, a pastor, a priest, and/or a family member that has truly only your best interest at heart. In getting help you will find the acceptance and forgiveness to move on and you will begin to love the problem away. This is how positive change becomes prolific. It is then when our insides begin to match our outsides.

You must gain control of your emotions. There are many ways to do this, but the true trick is to reoccupy the ownership of and regain complete power of your mind. This is your mind, this is your own territory: now claim it and control it so you have a happy existence.

This may sound easy, but it is harder than you might think. You need some tools to help you do this. We are going to explore some of these tools so you can take back your mind and take back your life!

The very first tool is evaluation. You must evaluate your life. Make peace with your past. What stories are you telling yourself that make you feel the way you do and are they true? What is in your life that is completely negative and dark that requires a true RESET? You need to kill those off. Death prompts us to live so kill off your fears which in

turn are the dead branches of your tree of your life so you are prompted to live freely. Forgive your past. Forgive your fears. Forgive yourself.

**Love=Freedom**
**Love=Peace**
**Love=Courage**
**Love=Life**

*"I am no longer and example of my circumstances*
*I have learned to rise above them."*

—JJ

Start over with love! I have had to kill off my idea of my personal and business relationships and what my life would look like a few times now because of the results of where the relationships were going. They were deeply affecting my emotions. I had to face the shame and deal with the disappointments and missed opportunities. They were affecting everything in my life and I had to realize each time that dream and that idea was dead. It was over. I needed to let it go. It was poisoning me by affecting my spirit, soul and body. We need to understand our emotions but learn to not be ruled by them. I needed to grieve, move through the pain, cry a lot, and find the strength which I never feel like having, but somehow I manage in order to move forward and write a new story for myself.

What is your best story? What is the story you want to live? We must remember we are all connected. All of us are the sum total of our experiences, and while of course we may react to them, we need to learn how to react like an evolved person and not our nine-year-old selves. Remind yourself that you are not that nine-year-old self. It is so easy to get caught up in your emotions that you forget who you are.

You lose perspective. Love that nine-year-old self and tell it its okay because they are safe and you are taking care of all things now with love. We must create a new story. A beautiful happy new story!

- Take a moment and pause here. Write down what you *want* your story to be. Imagine your problems are solved and you can step into the life you desire. What does that look like?

- What story do you want to tell yourself now?

- What do you want your life to look like after your RESET?

Even if you do not feel this way right now, I want you to say to yourself, "I am no longer an example of my circumstances. I have learned to rise above them. There is nothing else I can do other than love myself. Even when I feel terrible and sad I push forward and I thank God, I ask God why He is giving me this moment this pain." The truth is when you are going through the heartache of a breakup, a death, end of a job, end of a friendship … all the positive stuff people say to you is nice, but it feels like a bunch of B.S. What's real is that it takes time for your emotions to move through the pain.

As I was writing I had moments I would read what I wrote and know it was true, but even I had days when I felt like, "I can't do this I need to cry, I need to lock myself in the bathroom and cry!" In fact, I did this countless times on the set of Mobwives. RESET is hard! Processing your emotions is difficult, but necessary if you are to push through the pain and realize the benefits of healing and wholeness which await you.

This is a tough pill to swallow, but the grace in this is that there is someone who will love you with all your heart … and that person is you. Find your wholeness. Sew yourself back together with your own love. This is better anyway because you can choreograph this dance however you like. You are creating your own song of life and its yours to live however you please with grace, love, and happiness. When you are whole you have a whole lot of love to give to others, which in turn you will receive a ton of it. When you are depleted you are a dry energy source that becomes like dark, stagnant, murky water that eventually you cannot even see through. Find your light and follow it, even if it is just a glimmer and you will walk towards a lot happier emotions. Eventually they will take over and you will be that person you are forcing yourself and working towards becoming. You will learn to rule your emotions and not have them rule your life.

Letting Go!

*"When someone makes you that happy
remember they can make you that sad too."*

—JJ

When you change your thoughts, you change your situation. When you change your situation, you begin to see a shift in your circumstances. Your thoughts become your reality, so you must learn to think on purpose. Think about the future you desire. Think about a healthy body, think about a healthy bank account, healthy relationships, a healthy soul. You become what you think.

*"Don't let the silence be so loud that it
drives you crazy. Talk back to it!"*

—JJ

The moments when you are alone is when the quiet seeps in like a black thick fog of depression, sadness, and uncertainty. The silence can be so loud it can literally drive you crazy. These are the hardest moments to sit with and walk through. When going through a RESET, there will be times when a vibration of sadness fills you up and penetrates up and down your heart, up and down it goes, up and down the sadness rises and lowers just like the strings of a harp. It is in these moments of our darkness and in our sadness that we must find that mustard seed of inner strength and not reach for something negative to fill the void, but instead to move through the pain with hope and faith that God has something greater planned for us. What He has will illuminate us with so much happiness that it will actually cover the dark time, until it becomes a distant memory. It will become a memory of a how not to do it that way next time around, because if we do, we know the result is pain, and we know how that pain feels because we are feeling it now. Loneliness is the worse form of pain and sadness. It's a bitter fog that doesn't leave until we make it go. Quiet isn't always quiet, sometimes its very loud until we finally shut it off.

## REMEMBER:

*Healthy Emotions = Healthy Thoughts*

*Unhealthy Emotions = Poisonous Thoughts.*

*"Your thoughts and beliefs of the past have created this moment, and all the moments up to this moment. What you are now choosing to believe and think and say will create the next moment and the next day and the next month and the next year."*

—Louise L. Hay

Now you need a plan of attack! What can you do to start the healing? My friend asked me how I got through the pain? I answered, "First talk about your emotions and problems leading to these feelings. Find your why! Move the problem into a different space in your body and turn it into a strength. Find new solutions. Pray, meditate, practice inner empowerment so eventually you can help others."

In order to do that my other answer was, "Pay for encouragement, or find it and lots of it until you acquire new patterns of feelings, behaviors and reactions. I had a wonderful therapist, priest, pastor, yoga guru, trainer, Bible teacher, friends, family, and massage healer in my life. I know it sounds like a lot of different people, but I did everything and anything to arm myself with the knowledge to create a new foundation for myself so I could change, be empowered, and become the light to shine on others that God meant for me to be."

Even though I know God is always with me, sometimes in life or in a RESET my emotions take over and it does not feel like it's so. It feels lonely, sad and dark. It's so much easier to let the negative creep in as its almost effortless. Even positive people have to work to stay positive, but in the beginning of a RESET when your emotions are your enemy, finding the power to be positive is extremely hard. Even now when I am much healthier, when dark emotions creep in, I pull myself out of

the pit of hell and call my dear friend, a yoga guru, or go to church (which I do at least 2 to 3 mornings a week and on Sundays), or I call my friends. I have become disciplined in my faith, eating, and working out now, but I wasn't always. Adapting to these behaviors and routines has had an enormous effect on my emotions in a positive and fulfilling way. When in the pit of hell, search for the people who have words of encouragement. Ask God to help you and to help heal your heart.

> *"Just remember God is with you. Have I not commanded you? Be strong and courageous. Do not be afraid; do not be discouraged, for the LORD your God will be with you wherever you go."*
>
> —Joshua 1:9

So with that being said, it is not okay to be afraid anymore. It's time to get encouraged! Have a sound mind so you can be led out of your weakness and truly RESET your response to your emotions. Pay for encouragement, meditate, pray, and cry out to God and your answers will come. You will learn how to handle your emotions with a new mindset because with all your hard work you will be aligned with others who are healthy and positive. You will naturally borrow and implement their principles without even knowing and realizing it. Then all of a sudden you will be like, "Wow, I'm RESET!" Aligning with positive healthy people changes your mindset and is the best way to move forward.

Remember this: you attract what you are. I have done it a few times now. We attract a mirror reflection of ourselves to some extent. In my 20s I attracted a fun party boy because I was a fun, life-of-the-party girl. In my 30s I attracted someone loving but broken because I too was very loving and broken. Do you see the pattern here? This is why

getting a hold of your emotions is so important. It is so necessary to be pure and clean of all the after effects of the past, at least as much as possible, because you want to attract what serves your highest good, not the past that no longer serves you. Otherwise your emotions will still be shackled with pain and you will never be free of that in which you dutifully and willingly imprisoned yourself. You will always be wanting far more unless you take the time to work on yourself. Love yourself enough to trust that you truly and truthfully deserve the best.

There is truly a circle of life of energy as others help you, then you must help others and vice versa. That is a must as it is the purest way to serve God and to help yourself heal, transform, and live a fulfilled life. Maya Angelou said, "When you know better you do better." So please arm yourself with the know so you can DO! Your emotions will thank you.

## Endnotes

1.  *What is the Photograph of Frozen Water Crystals?* Masura Emoto. Retrieved from http://www.masaru-emoto.net/english/water-crystal.html.

2.  Ibid.

*"When you know better, you do better."*

—Maya Angelou

# Chapter Seven

# RESET—Finances

Disclaimer: I am not a financial counselor or financial expert. Please consult a professional to create a strategy that will work for you. This chapter on financial RESET is me sharing what worked for me. My desire for you is that you find something that will work for you to better your life forever.

*"My eyelashes are falling off and I have run out of money to glue them back on."*

—JJ

*"Failure is disguised as a fast forward to freedom."*
—JJ

*"If you don't listen to the red flags when they are waving they will soon enough hit you over your head."*

—JJ

Once upon a time I had money in reserve for emergencies. I once had security, now I had anxiety. My finances were in chaos. I was drowning in debt, burdened by responsibilities larger than my shoulders were ever designed to bear. I was dealing not only with my own consequences, but also the consequences from someone else's bad

judgment. I was paying someone else's way, enabling his bad behavior. He contributed bills without income and ran up debt on my accounts. The pile was so high I did not see how I could possibly work hard enough or long enough to take back my life.

> *"Tell me how you use your spare time and how you spend your money and I will tell you where and what you will be ten years from now."*
>
> —Napoleon Hill

I love this quote. Let's be real—if you are working like a dog, shopping, vacationing and keeping up with the Jones' guess what? When the Jones' are retiring guess where you will be? Not retiring! That's right you will still be working like a dog to pay for all that stuff you couldn't afford. Because you did not use any type of discernment or discipline to plan for your financial future, you will be stuck in the hamster wheel running and running but never getting anywhere! Now doesn't that stink?

It doesn't have to be that way. You can get it together. Small choices made today and sustained over time will change the picture dramatically. I was in a mess and worked my way out … you can too! Let's begin by asking some hard questions to find out where you are so you can make a plan to get where you want to be instead.

Use the Financial Stability Thermometer to help you see where you are and assess where you want to be. Knowledge is power. Denial will not get you out of debt. Facing what your situation actually is is the first step to getting a plan in place to change it to what you want it to become.

## Financial Stability Thermometer
### Figure 7.1

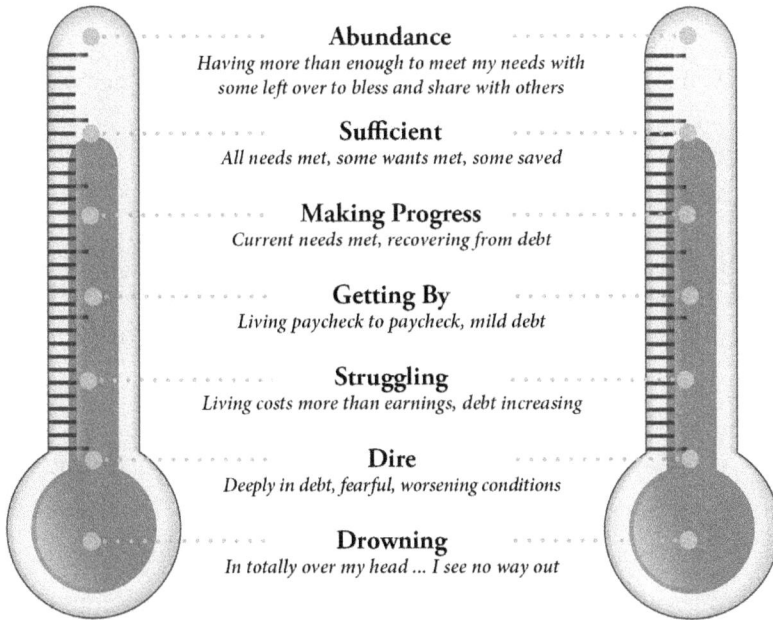

**Abundance**
*Having more than enough to meet my needs with
some left over to bless and share with others*

**Sufficient**
*All needs met, some wants met, some saved*

**Making Progress**
*Current needs met, recovering from debt*

**Getting By**
*Living paycheck to paycheck, mild debt*

**Struggling**
*Living costs more than earnings, debt increasing*

**Dire**
*Deeply in debt, fearful, worsening conditions*

**Drowning**
*In totally over my head ... I see no way out*

**Where I Am Now**                    **Where I Want To Be**

On the "Where I Am Now" thermometer, mark the category where you find your present financial condition. Only a hard, honest look at reality can prepare you for a Money RESET.

Now take a look at the "Where I Want to Be" thermometer and consider where you would like to find yourself in the future. It may seem impossible today, but it is not. There is hope ... your RESET awaits!

## Questions for Finances

   What is my financial normal? (For example: Is your normal a mortgage, multiple credit cards, living month-to-month making minimum payments while running up new charges? Are you a saver or spender?)

   What do I want my new financial normal to be?

   What does abundance look like to me?

- In what ways can I align myself to feel abundant?

- What is my big dream for my finances?

- What is my first financial goal for the RESET? What will help me feel successful?

- What timeline can I put on this goal to give it a deadline?

- Is my pride more important than my future?

*"What the mind can conceive it can achieve."*

—Napoleon Hill

Money is a funny thing. We need it to live. We need it to eat, sleep comfortably, clothe ourselves, and simply survive. But our ideas about money often become convoluted. Money ceases to be currency to do things to function and thrive. Money instead becomes an all encompassing and cumbersome thing. The pursuit of money often gets abused, leaving us exhausted not only physically, but spiritually too. We get trapped in our need for money. There never seems to be enough—no matter how much of it you actually have.

At the time I began my RESET, I was in a dire financial situation—I was in a dire life situation! To make progress I needed to remove some of the emotion and objectify the situation in front of me. I needed to see it in black and white, a true itemization of everything. I needed to dump some ice water over my head and wake the heck up!

Here is what I was facing:

- My relationship of over 10 years was over.

- I had to close my business once and for all because my new business partners had claimed bankruptcy. I was afraid if we

did not make serious, fast, and precise decisions we would be stuck with other debt from that business we might not even know we had. I was genuinely concerned that they may have attached us to debt we didn't know about. My franchise was no more. I had to say goodbye to that goal, that dream, that adventure. Goodbye!

ั All the hard work and money I had put into both businesses in the last seven years was gone, it was over! Panic and despair set in. I was traumatized. I could not see in front of me I was in a fog.

ั All I had to show for the last seven years was a closed business and debt. There was no equipment to sell—it had been devalued, no business property to sell, and my savings account was very low. Every time I made enough to put it back into my savings … boom! Something happened and I would have to dig into it again unwillingly, yet desperately.

ั I had serious business debt and a very hefty lifestyle with a lot of overhead.

ั The mortgage for the apartment I shared with my boyfriend was now in my name alone and the mortgage was large.

ั The taxes and condo fees were large—almost twice the monthly mortgage.

ั We had two cars. One of which was a Mercedes with a high payment. Insurance coverage was crazy expensive because of my (now ex) boyfriend/business partner's driving record.

ั I was the only one with a career. From the time we closed the business he did not work. He said he could not find a job,

but he spent his time drinking, sleeping, and playing on the computer. He contributing NOTHING financially to his own support. To this day he has never offered one dime to pay for business debt we incurred together.

- In order to store equipment I could not sell, I had to procure a rental unit. The cheapest I could find was still expensive. This left me with another expense for something that produced no income.

- I was paying for food, health insurance, utilities, pets (fish, birds, turtle, cats … ) and all the other expenses that come with life … on top of credit card debt. I was drowning!

One of the most emotional and awful decisions I had to make was finding a nice home for the beautiful birds that I had at the first spa. They were to go to the next spa, but that never happened because of the construction, so they were living in our apartment for almost a year. Getting rid of them was such a sad day in my life and I had to do it all alone. My boyfriend bailed on me that day and went to lunch to drink with our friend. I almost knocked myself out pulling that 4 foot tall cage down from the armoire while crying the whole time. I felt like such a horrible human being, but somehow I did it.

I found a beautiful home for them. They ended up in a home with a bird sanctuary. My beautiful friends who were my veterinarian and his lovely sister helped me find a home for our turtle as well. God is good and His grace carried me through! I loved my pets, but I was in a desperate situation. I think the act of knowing I could not give a living creature the best life possible and finding someone that could was an act of selfless love. Hard, selfless love. It was just plain awful!

# A Cold, Hard Look at the Facts

Desperate, I had no idea where to start cleaning up this mess. I began by taking a cold, hard look at the numbers. As I said, objectifying the situation. I knew if I allowed my emotions to overwhelm me, I would not find the courage to face the harsh reality and make the needed changes.

Following is a breakdown of all I had to look forward to. Understand, I paid these bills off in six years. It was a nightmare and probably the hardest thing I've ever done. I am being vulnerable with you here so you can see how deep I was in. Maybe you are in deep too, but if I came through it—you can too!

## JACQUI PHILLIPS LLC/ RELATIONSHIP FINAL BILLS

- ❧ I owed $11,268.00 to my business line of credit. I paid this off with my IRA. The fees and fines associated with it were $1,098.00 Federal Ira Penalty + $3,848.00 = $4,946.00. The grand total out of my pocket for this was **$16,214.00!**

- ❧ Though we owned our apartment jointly, the mortgage was in my name. After the break-up I had to turn this apartment into a rental property to save my butt. Here are the bills associated with this totaled = $25,243.26

- ❧ The total of all joint business expenses and partnership expenses including apartment bills = $93,021.82. My boyfriend had agreed to pay his half, making his share of the debt = $46,510.91. He paid $0.

I had been raised to use cash. I never used credit cards. I had them only because I knew I should have them to build credit. Even as a new college graduate living in NYC, I bought my furniture with cash!

While running our spa business, each time we were signing up for a new credit card or opening a credit line with the bank I got a sick feeling in the pit of my stomach. Dancing with credit produces children of debt. I knew this in my heart. I knew I was asking for trouble in my future. The voice of truth that comes from our higher self was whispering to me. It was shouting, "Hey! Hey ... hey! Listen to me! I am telling you this is not right, this doesn't feel right! Stop!"

> *"If you are honest people may cheat*
> *you. Be honest anyway."*
>
> Mother Teresa

I did not listen to the red flags so they eventually hit me over the head. When things do not feel right they are not! So why on earth was I making these bad and dangerous decisions that would haunt me for years? I didn't want to, but I felt trapped. Believing the situation was temporary was less painful than actually getting off the ride. Boy was I wrong! It wasn't until I ripped off that bandaid that the wound could breath and heal. It took me four years to figure that little tidbit out ... but at last I knew the truth!

Have you ever gotten yourself in a situation you realize you may have never wanted? That was the spa for me. Even from the very beginning I remember being in the UK on tour and having a drink at the hotel bar with the guys in the band and talking to the bartender. Eventually, another drink or two later I told him the story of how I was having second thoughts. I remember him saying, "Just back out." I answered, "It's too late ... construction has started!" This was happening whether I liked it or not.

I should have listened to my voice of truth. My spirit was literally screaming, warning me. "No, no, no, … this is a mistake. This is not your destiny. This is not your purpose!" Follow the checks in your spirit.

Hundreds of thousands of dollars literally went down the tube now after the fact. I wish now that I would have paused, prayed, and listened to the voice. The difference between now and then is now I have the tools. Now I know how to. Thank you, God. I humbly thank You!

Money Represents All Things

I realized money is an exchange of life. Every time I spent money, I was exchanging the currency of my life. How I spend my money is the truest representation of my values. They are reflected in my dollars.

## Dear Future Self...

As I went along, I made myself a list about some legal things to do in finance matters in business and relationships that I wish I would have done and did not! This list is not comprehensive, but it may help you avoid some of the pitfalls I endured.

## PROPERTY:

When buying property with another person: husband, lover, or boyfriend—think of all the ramifications to make sure that no matter what happens, could it be maintained? Basically, are you prepared for the what ifs. Things such as:

- Loss of job, or business

- Death

- Breakup or ending of the relationship

## BANK ACCOUNTS:

A-Z, keep one of your own. Be in control of your own money. Even if you share equally (which many couples do and can be perfectly wonderful and healthy), but know what is going on. Be in the know! The "know" is your power! Not power like psycho-

power and control, but power like "I know what the heck is going on in my life, our life, my world, our world therefore I am confident at the decisions being made and feel comfortable with them."

If there are uncomfortable situations, then at least you have the opportunity to speak your piece and quite possibly deter a bad decision being made on your behalf that you could regret for a long drawn out torturous time! At the end of the day feeling powerful and empowered is good for a relationship. Feeling powerless is not. Make sure you have healthy boundaries about money. Decide together and communicate openly about what is and is not in bounds!

## BILLS:

Is your name on everything? Are both of your names on everything? Who is responsible if the bills are not paid? Who will carry the burden of debt incurred? Is the burden shared legally?

These are important facts to know especially if the relationship ends. Who gets stuck with debt you made while together? Don't be a dummy like me! This school of thought can be the same for partnerships. Many loved ones go into business together, believing that relationship will keep everyone honest and have each other's highest and best interests at heart. I don't care if it is your husband, brother, sister, or lover, this naïve optimism can make you broke!

## RETIREMENT PLAN:

Have one. Have your own. Take care of yourself. Think of your future self. Do you want to sleep in someday or work until the day you die?

## CARS:

While there can be many benefits to having a car owned in both names, it can also be good to have your own car in your own name. There are some good reasons for this choice as well. It is good for your credit, it is good for your spirit, and great for your independence. Not only that, but if you need to leave the relationship, it is much easier if you don't have a jointly owned asset.

## CHECK YOUR CREDIT OFTEN:

I had a bad experience. Before my second RESET, he wiped out one of my mom's bank accounts that she allowed him access to. Behind my back and without my knowledge, he had her take out two loans in her name. My business coach/therapist had me run my credit and monitor it to see if anything had been done in my name as well. I now do this often and get alerts as we should in this world of online madness.

This can easily happen in relationships, especially when the mail is shared. It is easy to open a card in someone else's name. Luckily, this did not happen and my credit was still excellent, but you must be careful. Be proactive and protect yourself. Remember the three P's: **Proactive People Progress!** I would

rather prevent then resent. Do yourself a favor and keep that in mind and it will save you a lot of headaches!

> *"Break up with your business before*
> *it breaks up with you."*
>
> —JJ

> *"Plans fail for lack of counsel, but with*
> *many advisers they succeed."*
>
> Proverbs 15:22

I held on too long. Choosing bad partners in business and bad lovers was a detriment to my life for years. It forced me to have to close one business and bankrupt another business. A lawyer, several accountants, and CEO friends advised me to do this. Though I was adamantly against this and fought it for a few years, I was literally just treading very murky water.

Even though the business I owned went belly up, I was still on the hook for things I had personally guaranteed for the business. "If the business can't pay for it then it is not getting it," should have been my motto, but it wasn't. This created one of the lowest, most regretful, embarrassing times of my life. I felt and believed I was a failure. People say, "It's just business," but to me it was personal.

That "just business" had my name on it. I killed myself for years trying to make a go of it. Because of the lack of effort on my partner and his absolute resistance to get a job when the ceiling collapsed, my hand was forced. Business bankruptcy was the last resort and one I will always regret, but I regret with gratitude because I learned this lesson!

# Wheel of Power & Control
### Figure 7.2

Not all abuse is violent. Many times a RESET is needed because of the repeated manipulation and control of a toxic relationship.

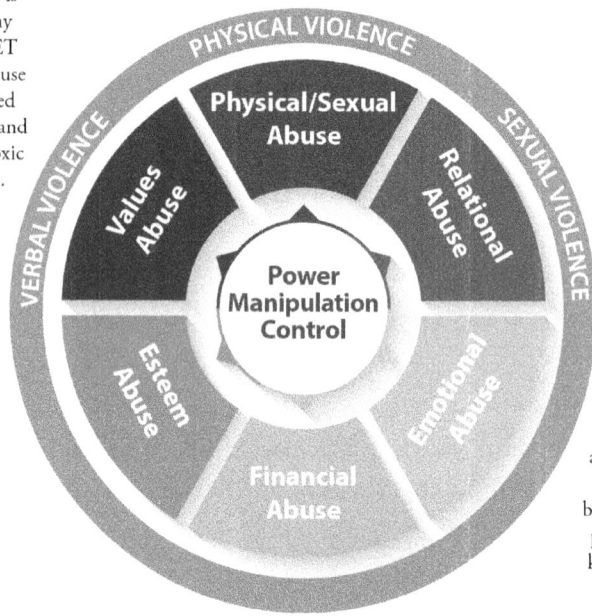

PHYSICAL VIOLENCE

**Physical/Sexual Abuse**

Values Abuse

SEXUAL VIOLENCE

Relational Abuse

VERBAL VIOLENCE

**Power Manipulation Control**

Esteem Abuse

Emotional Abuse

**Financial Abuse**

Learn to spot abusive patterns and set healthy boundaries which protect you and keep you strong.

## Physical/Sexual Abuse

Intimidation: threatening looks, actions, gestures, words
Threats: breaking things, abusing pets
Seizing Control: forcing sex, forcing servitude
Physical violence: hitting, choking, bruising, restraining

## Financial Abuse

Prevent her from getting or keeping a job
Putting debt in her name, against her credit
Stealing money: depleting savings, borrowing from her friends or family with no payback
Handling all money: refuse her access to account information, status, bills, etc.

## Relational Abuse

Isolation: controlling who she sees, where she goes, what she does, what she watches or reads
Limits her activities: she must get permission to do anything without him
Jealousy: absorbing her focus

## Esteem Abuse

Minimizing her worth, putting her down
Making her feel no one else would have her
Calling her ugly names, insulting her appearance
Making her feel she is nothing without him

## Emotional Abuse

Mind Games: making her feel crazy or stupid
Passive/Aggressive Behavior
Threatening suicide or harming himself
Threatening to take away children, or turning children against her
Blame: making her feel responsible for abuse

## Values Abuse

Belittling things she holds dear—her beliefs, her faith, her values
Putting himself ahead of her at all times
Keeping her from attempts at personal growth, self-help, education, or improvement

# *Money Abuse*

Not all abuse is violent. As you saw in the illustration for the Wheel of Power & Control, financial manipulation in a relationship is another form of abuse. It is toxic. The economic abuse of women who earn high levels of income is on the rise. Once in a relationship, the abuser depletes the woman financially, victimizing her through entrapment, making her feel responsible to take care of his needs,

> *Financial manipulation is another form of abuse.*

manipulating her desire to nurture. Too often a woman finds herself hopelessly in debt, totally entangled in the financial distress of a partner and unsure how to get free. I was that woman. I needed to escape financial abuse and it was hard to face.

In my experience with relationships I have loved working together, sharing, and empowering each other and rise to the occasion both in business and in the relationship. But what happens when the other person gives up and drops the ball? What happens when that other person refuses to work or pull their fair share? What happens when the other person abuses the money you make? What happens when you get into a relationship where you have jointly agreed to work and pay bills together, and then it all comes to a screeching halt? When does having compassion for your loved one turn into being used, abused and taken advantage of?

A situation like this becomes abusive. This kind of stress and burden can cause many problems. I often joked that I had Post Traumatic Stress Disorder (PTSD).

PTSD is a disorder that develops in some people who have seen or lived through a shocking, scary, or dangerous event. While I would

never equate what I experienced with what soldiers face on a battlefield, the trauma I endured was real and painful.

It is natural to feel afraid both during and after a traumatic situation. Fear triggers many split-second changes in the body to help defend against danger or to avoid it. This "fight-or-flight" response is a healthy reaction meant to protect a person from harm. Nearly everyone will experience a range of reactions after trauma, yet most people recover from initial symptoms naturally. Those who continue to experience problems may be diagnosed with PTSD. People who have PTSD may feel stressed or frightened even when they are not in danger.

As women we are natural caretakers. We truly feel it is our duty and our desire to love unconditionally. This natural maternal instinct to sacrifice our own good for the protection of others can get twisted and used against us. How do we learn when to stop? Where to draw the line? How do we break this cycle when we are in an abusive and dangerous situation?

Roles in society have changed dramatically. Women are now doing everything: being not only a wife and mother, but often also the main breadwinner. This places an enormous amount of stress on a woman. Though I haven't personally looked at any research, I have often wondered if female hair loss and heart disease are not connected with this new role she has been asked to play.

If responsibilities with the home and household are shared, a woman as the breadwinner is not a problem. However, if you are in a relationship with a man who feels entitled and has grown up being nurtured, cared for, and has had all his needs provided for … this can turn ugly fast! This is a new form of abuse: it is economic abuse.

Economic abuse is not just the traditional form as explained in the standard power and control wheel, because this type of abuse breeds a

lot of the other cousins of abuse such as emotional abuse, intimidation, and manipulation. The abuser will use children, threats, and isolation. An economic abuser will have his cake and eat it too. He'll watch you slave to death and convince you there is still more you should be doing for him. So please take this seriously and evaluate yourself to see if in fact you are going through this or if you recognize that someone you love is. It became painfully obvious to my friends and family long before I was willing to see the problem. In the end it was still up to me to act and deliver my freedom to myself!

> *"I may not be perfect for everyone but*
> *I AM PERFECT for someone and*
> *that someone starts with me."*
>
> —JJ

## Answer to Prayer

One thing I know how to do is work hard and make money! I also believe and know that the best way to be abundant and successful is by having multiple streams of income. So here I was in a serious jam, and out of the blue I was offered a job doing makeup for a morning show. Now we are talking about a really early commitment. It was a get out of bed daily at 4:00 AM to accept the job commitment. I already had a demanding schedule as I had a lot of other shows, one of which was Mobwives. This made for very long days, although great, still long! I thought about it, I prayed about it, and I knew in my heart if I said yes to work, the work would keep coming. I knew God would provide me the means and by this I would gain my freedom! When God says, "Hello," and you answer, He will open the door of new opportunity. So when the door of opportunity opened to work for the morning show and I answered, I realized that financial freedom really was on its way. I

got hungry to pay off everything and was willing to do whatever it took to be financially free again!

I had two options. I could bury my head in the sand like an ostrich and pretend the problem wasn't there. Perhaps if I just refused to look, maybe it would go away. Or, I could get high above the problem and get a view of the whole situation—use an eagle's eye to see a path out. I decided I wanted to spread my wings like an eagle and fly to freedom!

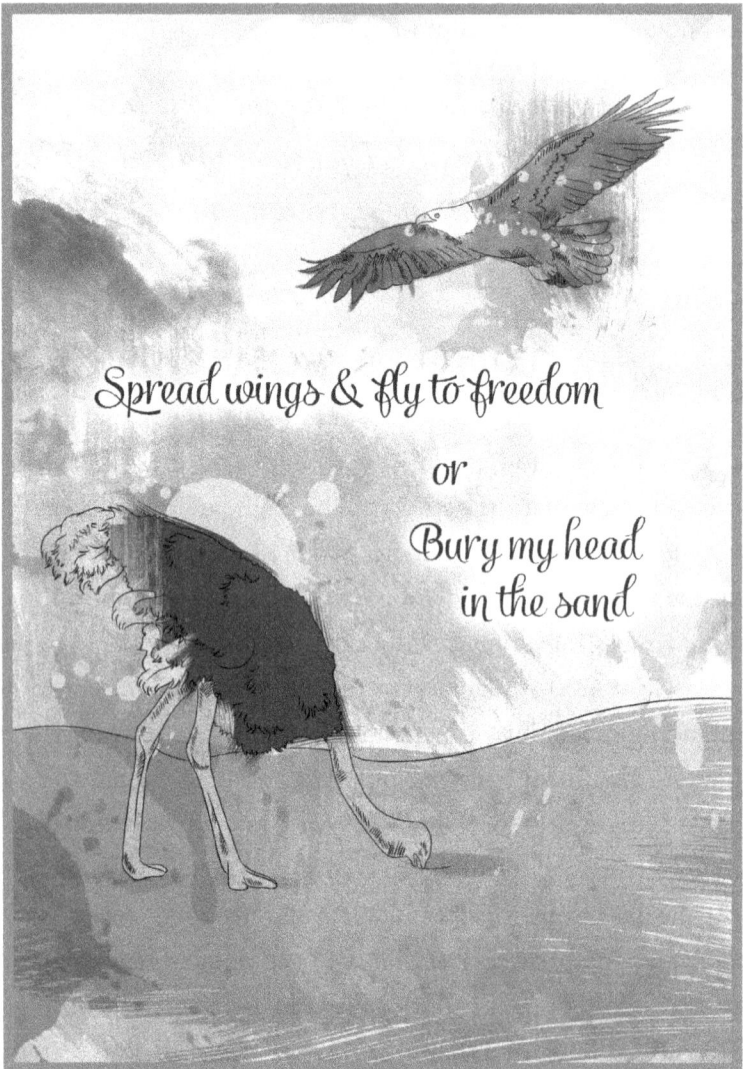

Spread wings & fly to freedom

or

Bury my head
in the sand

Everything has a price. I thought about what changing my schedule so drastically would mean in my life and how I could use it to my advantage. I thought about the fact that even though I was facing this insurmountable situation, this was a great plan of attack. By doing this job I could actually work before work. I could designate this money solely to paying off the business debt.

As I dedicated those funds to paying off debt, it allowed me a chance to dream again. I began to believe those dreams would be attainable. If I could work extra to retire debt, I could keep working extra to finance new dreams! I knew if I could provide myself this abundant mindset then I would flourish eventually. It would not and was not easy, but it was doable and I am so grateful to God for this opportunity. This morning show gave me a new-found discipline which in turn completely changed my life for the good!

> *"There is an abundance of everything for the person who knows what he wants."*
> —Napoleon Hill

My plan of attack was made from a variety of things, but first I really paused and prayed. I thought long and hard about my options all that there was to consider. I had to face, "How the heck am I gonna pay almost $100,000 of business debt off when that business was closed and producing no income?"

I knew I had to make serious sacrifices. I knew my changes needed to come in leaps and bounds. At the time I was bringing in a decent income. If I had not had the debt, it was a nice living. But I was tired— no, make that exhausted! I was doing this all on my own. Facing the regular responsibilities of living on a single income WITH the added pressure of a mountain of business debt I had to grapple with all on my own.

From working at CNBC that feeding myself with education by simply listening and reading was priceless. I knew from an author and talent that I had the pleasure of working with, Lynette Khalfani Cox, to attack debt one credit card at a time. I chose the little ones first to build confidence, but I also put bigger than minimum payments on the large ones. I allocated money accordingly. I moved out of my beautiful high-rise apartment and got a tenant as a nice big way to lower my monthly living overhead and crush the debt even faster. I looked at all the ways that I could cut spending and dedicated extra money to the task at hand. I quit flying to Pittsburgh to see my family as much and started taking the Megabus, which I must say was kind of delightful because it was cheap and easy. Who knew? The plus and upside in this was that now I could come home a lot instead of sometimes because it was so affordable.

This was truly my course in miracles and money management/ empowerment. I had ended a bad relationship that left me in this state, but before long was in another one. During this time of paying off debt, my new boyfriend was borrowing a lot of money from me. Apparently, I had not yet learned my lesson. Because I did not break up with my Stronghold Family, they came a knocking. Yes, it was in a different form, but it was still attacking my weakness, my vulnerability to help others even if it meant hurting myself. This is wrong and this woman today would not do that because I have the tools and I am equipped with a different kind of self love that gives me the right discernment to know the difference from right and wrong choices for me!

Anyway, even though that was happening I was still able to pay off the debt in six years. I got a shot to produce my first QVC product for

a contest I was in, and also produce my show *Stars Behind The Stars*. Learning how to allocate money was key and acting like you don't have it is also key because it causes you learn to live a more humble and cost efficient life. I also rebuilt my savings to have 12 months of income for the "just in case" scenario, so I feel abundant! Feeling abundant is the first step of true empowerment because it creates an energy of momentum that will help you propel forward and inspire you to achieve your goals!

# Living Abundantly

Looking back, yes, it was all crazy but going for it and "taking it like a man" was the best decision of my life. My new schedule created a discipline that allowed me to get up, go to work before other work, go to church, meditate, go to the gym, and then continue about my day. These positive habits have created abundantly positive outcomes.

Dr. Wayne Dyer always talks about paying attention to when you are most inspired and I learned through all this that my inspiration is best in the morning. I have my most creative thoughts and I am definitely connected to God and the Holy Spirit the most in the morning. It is when I hear Him best. So I encourage you to pay attention to the time you will be most productive and that is when you should work on your RESET goals as they will be more attainable and will flow better. Find your best time of day to truly align with God and His Spirit so your productive energy will flow easily. I cannot express enough how super important it is to create a space of time just for you to sow into yourself and plant the seeds of education and renewal.

Knowledge is power. It gives us the courage and tools to act. It is also so important to really educate yourself and arm yourself with that

power because those are the tools of reinforcement that will allow you to push through and continue to reinvent yourself until you are truly walking in your purpose and destiny.

Personally I love reading and listening to Napoleon Hill, learning and living that abundance is a mindset. But it can be a challenge. When we are surrounded by darkness, training our brains to have that mindset of abundance and getting rid of our limiting beliefs can be difficult. This is when isolation and negativity kicks in. I have learned through my Bible studies and through all the other experts I study that an abundant mindset while not only takes faith, it is also like a muscle that we must be committed to working on the same as we do with our diet and exercise.

Thoughts are things like the great Louise Hay teaches us. They are real and the more we think things, the faster they manifest into the physical form. Be careful and mindful of your thoughts because they will become your reality. The brain believes what you think the most. Rewire your brain for success. Start thinking happy and abundant thoughts and watch your miracles unfold! Now don't you want happy to come true? Keep your eyes on the present and future, not the past. Do not be intimidated by your present reality, put your eyes on a brighter goal.

> *Your thoughts become your reality. The brain believes what you think the most.*

Learn to become present in this moment. God puts you into places and spaces where He can shift your paradigm and cause you to think differently. Honor this. Your miracle financial breakthrough often comes while you are in the midst of being faithful with what you have. God will provide a way through for you. When He asks, answer!

*"Treat money the way you want it to treat you. If you want it to love you for a long time, then you need to nurture it. This means saving, investing in it, and working on the relationship so it grows. It's the same with people, and it's the same with health. It is also the same with self love. Work on it, invest your time and energy toward positive outcomes—believe in the positive outcome and that outcome will manifest itself into physical form."*

—JJ

*"Money can be your best friend or your worst enemy. It's your choice, you decide."*

—JJ

# Chapter Eight

# RESET—Appearance

> "If you're sad add more lipstick and attack."
>
> —Coco Chanel

> "Beauty is in your heart and soul, not
> in the eye of the beholder."
>
> —JJ

## Bloom!

**BLOOM = BELIEVE LOVE OF OURSELVES MATTERS!**

> *Your beauty should not come from outward
> adornment, such as elaborate hairstyles and
> the wearing of gold jewelry or fine clothes.
> Rather, it should be that of your inner self, the
> unfading beauty of a gentle and quiet spirit,
> which is of great worth in God's sight.*
>
> 1 Peter 3:3-4

## Appearance Thermometer
### Figure 8.1

**I Love Me!**
*Oh, you sexy thang!*
*It just doesn't get any better than this!*

**Look Awesome, Feel Great!**
*I am healthy, strong, and fit*

**Good As It's Gonna Get ...**
*I don't love my body, but this is the best I can do*

**Not Terrible**
*Not really fat, but not fit—not bad enough to change*

**Ordinary**
*Pleasantly plump, the right wardrobe hides my sins*

**I Feel Unattractive**
*I hate mirrors, hate trying on clothes, feel fat*

**I Feel Ugly**
*I am body conscious, I have a negative self image,*
*I feel people judge me for my size & appearance*

**Where I Am Now**                              **Where I Want To Be**

On the "Where I Am Now" thermometer, mark the category which best describes how you feel about your appearance. Honesty sets you up for a successful Appearance RESET.

Now take a look at the "Where I Want to Be" thermometer and consider where you would like to find yourself in the future. Mark this is also so you can begin to chart your course to reach this important goal!

## Questions for Appearance:

1. Does your appearance reflect your passion? Do you dress for success? Does your personal style match the life you want or the life you have settled for?

2. When do you remember feeling the most attractive and confident about your appearance? When do you remember

feeling the least attractive and most insecure about your appearance? Why?

3. Is your appearance current or outdated? (Hair, makeup, clothing, accessories, nails, etc.)

4. Do you feel like you have a personal style? If yes, do you feel confident about your personal style?

5. What changes do you need to make in your personal style to reflect how you want to appear?

Your appearance guides your possibilities. Show up dressed for the part you want to play! Dress for your life, look like you want to feel—it will make you feel better.

If you are sleepwalking through your life, then chances are your style and appearance are also pretty tired-looking. Don't feel bad, we are all guilty of it at times especially during a RESET! This is the time to stop hitting the snooze button, wake up and be fabulous! If you were going to run in a race you would make sure to wear the right shoes right? Why don't you do the same with your appearance for the rest of your life? Your costume, your "on camera look" for this movie we call life is important. Do we not want to put our best face forward?

You look how you feel, or at least you see yourself that way. I have experienced this a lot in my life. Especially since I am a very sensitive and emotional person. It truly doesn't really matter at all how I actually look: how thin I am, how fat I am, how young I am, how old I am etc. I *feel* thin or fat, young or old, therefore, in my mind that's how I look. What matters to me is how I feel because that translates into how I present myself. I remember once I was speaking at an event and I was so sad that day. My heart was broken. I kept trying to talk myself into being positive, I mean I should have been happy to have such a

nice opportunity in my life, but I just could not shake how my heart was feeling. I was so sad, I couldn't stop crying. I literally did my false eyelashes in the car so I had the drive to get it together and get my eyes dry enough to glue those puppies on! The reason I am telling you this is because sometimes we can not shake how we feel. Sometimes we have to fake it.

Pretend you are feeling fabulous by looking that way! The funny thing is that particular day I was speaking about inspiration. In the depths of my soul I truly believed in everything I was going to share, but at that moment I did not feel it for myself. All I could think of and could not get out of my head was, "Why is this love over? How could something so beautiful, soulful and promising be so fleeting?" I need love to breathe. At least I thought I did. I mean who am I kidding, I do! It is the oxygen that fills my soul and spirit. My love, my sunlight was gone and it showed … at least to me when I looked in my eyes I saw the sorrow that was resonating there transmuted into the pain I was feeling. I wondered when I would get my light back?

Appearance can be altered to reflect that of what we **want** to be. If we present it, we will eventually "be it." The funny thing is that everyone came up to me that day and said, "You look really great!" The whole time I wanted to say, "If only you knew how I really feel, because I would really like to get the heck out of here, go home, lay in my bed, and cry." I am a professional makeup artist, I know how to fake my appearance—most people do not.

So with this being said, please don't judge someone's sad appearance as most likely its a mirror into their soul. I'm not talking about the no makeup and gym clothes look when you are running to the store, I am talking about repetitive, sad, sorrowful looks. Sometimes people do not look good on the outside because they feel awful on the inside. Don't

be fooled, be kind instead. When you lose your love for life you feel like you lose your beauty, or smarts or strength—it's different for all of us. One thing is for sure, this is when your outsides are dreadful and they match the condition of your insides, it is time for some healing! The only way to move through this is to surrender and then rise up with God. They say time heals all wounds. It isn't true. It will take time, but we must allow God to do the work to heal our hearts.

*Bloom into Beautiful!*

## "Believe Love Of Ourselves Matters
## B-L-O-O-M into Beautiful!"

Words are powerful! They stick with us. They either build us up or they haunt our spirits. Some words resonate deeply. They attach themselves to our inner mind. This inner mind world and dialogue can continue to make us sad and break our hearts over and over which in turn leaves us looking (at least for me) and feeling ugly. The way you feel about yourself affects the way you look at and view yourself. You may gain weight or you may lose weight, but when I am hurting and feeling deep pain, my beauty is lost. I feel ugly, old, and washed up! Its not so much the physical beauty as it is the spiritual beauty. We lose our joie de vie. Our joy of life is gone! The glow of being in love, in love with life and just plain happy fades. The sparkle of the eye, the glowing skin I know at times I have lost this and I feel like a shell, an imposter occupying my own body.

God just wants us to love Him. We show that love by loving ourselves. He made us in his image, therefore should we not love what He made. If we don't love ourselves, why not? It is only natural that we want to make our parents happy and they are happy by seeing us succeed. So why wouldn't our Father in heaven want us to be happy also? We do that by excelling, by being happy, and taking care of ourselves. That includes looking good and feeling great!

## Jacqui's Professional Makeup Tips to Look Fabulous

My profession has allowed me to learn many helpful tricks and tips to looking fabulous—which goes a long way in helping you feel fabulous.

These are awesome tips, but at the end of the day, it must be your belief that you are beautiful that takes over. If you believe it, then you are. Your perception of you is what matters. I encourage you to make the effort to look your best when you need to so you simply feel good and perform your best!

## BEAUTY AND CREATING YOUR BEST SELF

*You are altogether beautiful, my darling; there is no flaw in you.*

Song of Songs 4:7

### *FACE:*

*Prep, Prime, Primp:* Wash your skin thoroughly. Use toner if needed. Make sure no makeup residue is on your skin. Use a moisturizer, primer, concealer, and foundation. Use concealer under the eyes and wherever it is necessary to cover blemishes and disguise any redness or discoloration. Blend all makeup thoroughly and do not forget the neck. Harsh lines from foundation, eyeshadow, blush, and even eyebrows will make you look like an amateur. Blending is your most important step, please take the time to do it properly. I use my fingers, a brush, and a sponge to get the best results and create the most natural, polished look.

### *EYEBROWS:*

Eyebrows are so important they are in a league of their own. Eyebrows frame the face and open up the eyes. They truly give us the lift we need to create beautiful eyes. Always make sure to apply with small strokes no matter what the product is such as powder, pencil, gel or a little of everything and always brush through each time with a spoolie brush.

## CONTOUR/HIGHLIGHT:

Contouring is a must for makeup application for pictures, a big day or media, and it's the oldest trick in the book. Every person has different contour needs, but the general rule of thumb is to create a more defined bone structure to your face in order to make the makeup pop! Especially when you're on or in front of a camera, you want to use contouring skills to define your cheekbones, temples, forehead, neckline (don't forget to blend), and nose if needed. Then you will want to highlight your cheekbones, perhaps the middle of the nose, cupids bow above the lip, a little under the eyes and under your eyebrows. By doing both contouring and highlighting it creates a better defined and balanced look for your face.

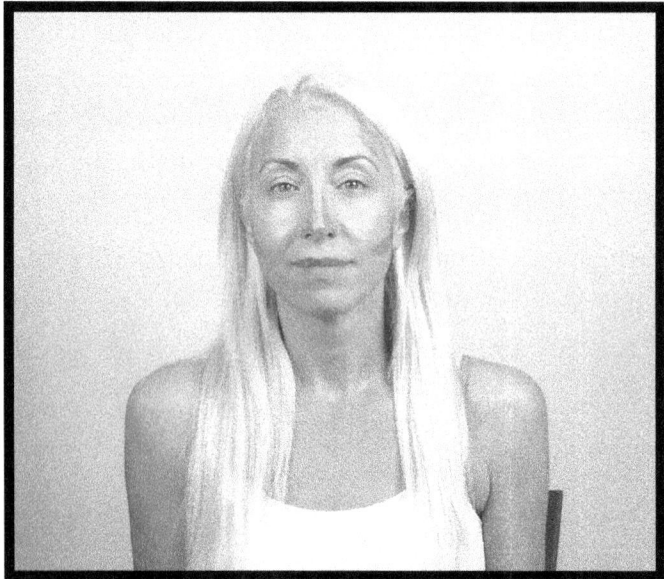

Makeup for photos in this section by Laura Koski at Doll Cosmetics
Photo by Chris Elia Luppo

## EYES AND LASHES:

Eye makeup is a personal experience. Period. It does not need to be perfect, but it does need to be blended. The easiest way to do your own eyeshadow is to create an even palette first by using concealer as your eyeshadow primer. Then go over the whole eye with a nude color, or a champagne, etc. to create a lighter and blended palette that is prepped. I usually look in the mirror with my eye a little open to create the contour. My favorite trick is to go above the contour area with a little pink, coral or mauve to create a more tiered blended effect. This way the eye is nicely blended and does not look harsh. The best way to enhance your eyes is by wearing false eyelashes. I prefer to always line the eyes first, then apply the lashes, then go over the line again. Once you are done take a look and do some final blending above and below the eyes. I always love to accentuate the inner corners of the eyes with a little highlight of white, gold, or champagne. This is a great trick!

## *LIPS:*

Lips are a very important part of your face as people are looking at them. When you are talking, your lips are front and center, so please do not forget to touch them up as they are what really pull the look together! Always accentuate them with a little pop of color as it really helps make your look polished. Also now that you have put such hard work in making your makeup so beautiful, please have lipstick and or lipgloss on at all times as it will make you look washed out if you do not. This is very important!

## *BODY:*

Please look over your chest, arms, hands and legs for any blemishes or discoloration. I often apply makeup to my clients hands because a lot of times the hands are lighter than their faces or we are muting the veins a bit. Please be considerate of this for yourself—you will be glad you did.

## *LAST THOUGHT:*

As women in the world we leave a stamp on many people. There is an unconscious motivation of confidence that exudes us while we are putting ourselves out there in the public eye. With that being

said, please remember to go out in the world with love and offer the world YOUR BEST YOU!

## WHAT ABOUT THE WARDROBE?

Does your appearance reflect your passion? Do you dress for success? Do you dress and embody the life you want or the life you have settled for? Unfortunately this does matter people. Forbes magazine did a study and appearance not only gets you the job sometimes, but you also earn more. So I ask you, what part are you dressing for? Are you dressing to be a teacher, a business woman, a mother, or how about just simply dressing for success? This includes your beauty too, not just clothes. We all view success and beauty differently. It means something different to each and every one of us which is great, but there is a common thread that is running through the vein of success and that is effort! So are you making effort to look and feel good?

I am guilty of not looking good, especially when I am working as a makeup artist. I am the chef that does not cook at home, and the shoemaker without shoes! Unfortunately, and I am just keeping it real, when I was working on Mobwives as the Makeup Department Head for six seasons it was like family. I would have shown up in my pajamas, (which, I am not saying who but one girl did more than once)! It was not right that I quit making an effort, but I did. I was going through a RESET. I was emotional, sad, and I just simply didn't care. I felt like just getting out of bed was an accomplishment, I had no energy for more. As I worked toward my RESET, I started to lose weight, felt good, and made an effort to wear a little makeup. Guess what? You guessed it ... I met the next boyfriend once I got my groove back.

Looking back, I should have always made the effort because this affected so many other things in my life. My other projects were

stagnant —a direct result of how I was feeling about myself and the on-and-off-again effort I gave life instead of a rocket-ship-effort that made strides daily. So whether we want to admit it or not, how we feel about ourselves impacts how we look at ourselves. This is reflected in the way we present ourselves and speaks volumes to our confidence which influences the results we see in our performance in all areas of our life!

I didn't go to school for makeup. I have a degree in Criminology, but I learned my craft from people doing it on me as a model and me having to do it for myself. I always did have a knack for makeup. I did my first wedding when I was 11 years old for my cousin! Isn't it funny how when we are children, before life has piled up the layers, our passion is often right near the surface, in plain site, begging to be developed. Through the years I learned the art by simply trying. When something worked great, I did it again. When it didn't I learned my lesson and didn't do it again! You too can do this and become your own fashion guru!

I think the reason I have been successful as a Celebrity Makeup Artist and always worked so much is because I share my heart and love with others. Even when I don't feel like it and people are acting crazy I try to be kind, a beacon of light, and offer up my highest self (most times), and then I do my best to give love. This has been a key to my success. With that in mind, I ask you these questions:

1. Do you offer your highest self on a daily basis?

2. Do you offer love to the world? At home? At work?

3. Do you have patience with others? When you do not how do you handle it?

4. Are you a good friend to yourself? Are you kind? Do you take good care of you or are you at the bottom of your list?

# *Mirror, Mirror*

Many people stand before a mirror, looking into it and say kind things and repeat mantras to themselves. It works. It helps you. You believe what you hear yourself say out loud. There is also danger in this practice. As someone who has spent the last 15 years in front of a mirror for sometimes 12 hours or more a day at a time working as a makeup artist in media, I know how powerful "mirror talk" can be. What happens if you don't like what you are looking at? You say terrible things to yourself about yourself. You focus on every flaw and magnify it. You blow them out of proportion until it is all you can see. Then you project that negative self image to everyone you meet until you have poisoned their view of you as well.

Making an effort with your appearance will make you feel better. When you feel better it shows. People respond to you differently, so you feel even better. So if you make an effort you will start to like what you see and your appearance will, in fact, start to reflect your passion and not the life you have settled for. I have been witness to this almost every day of my life because when someone walks into hair and makeup they often look like they just rolled out of bed. Let's face it, they have! But by the time I am done working on them, it is truly like a different person is born right before my eyes. Their new look, new face, new attitude, new persona exudes and even their body is new because the confidence is completely evident in their posture. They literally turn into a beautiful butterfly before my eyes. It's that simple. Often times they work through whatever is going on internally with me and that helps too, to talk about it. So what if you don't have someone like me to be your therapist and make you beautiful and feel it inside and out? I recommend meditation: saying positive things to yourself and believing them to be true. I also recommend exercise. It

clears my head and makes my skin glow! You can be your own beauty guru with a little effort. Effort = Exuberance. First impressions matter, so make a good one!

Your RESET in your appearance is another great opportunity to use your I Am Statement. Say to yourself. "I Am Beautiful, I Am Flawless, I Am Love, I Love Me, I Love All Of ME!" Use these statements, believe them, and embody them. They work!

## APPEARANCE MATTERS

According to *Forbes* tall people get paid more money. The article cited a 2004 study at the University of Florida that showed for every inch of height, a tall worker earns an average of $789 more per year!

*Tall, thin people make more money.*

The same article shared that fat people are paid less, and obese women are at the biggest disadvantage (and being an obese caucasian woman has the largest wage penalty). Women with a body mass index above 30 are paid an average of $8,666 per year LESS than their thin coworkers. Obese men are paid an average of $4,772 per year less than slimmer counterparts. In addition, obesity is also a factor in discrimination for hiring and raises.

Forbes went on to say that blonde women are paid more than female employees with any other color of hair. (Is that crazy or what?) Other factors that affect earning are exercise, (yep, those who work out regularly get paid higher than couch potatoes), and women who wear makeup earn as much as 30% more than women who do not wear makeup. Being attractive is apparently, attractive!

## A BIG MISTAKE

I learned ugly way too early in life! I remember being a very young girl and the exact moment I decided to cut all my hair off. I remember how I plotted and bribed my cousin to drive me to the hair salon and lying to her that my mom had allowed me to get a perm. You see I was suffering. My PapPap had died, my parents were getting a divorce, my mom and I were moving into a little apartment, and my Catholic School was shutting down because of radiation on the grounds. Everything I knew was over! I was so miserable, I needed a change and I felt if I cut off all my hair and looked pretty (like my much older cousin who I looked up too) I would feel better. I thought by chopping off my hair I would lose all the weight I was feeling—the heaviness of life. I had it all figured out. I had money and I was a master manipulator I would get it done ... and I was eight years old!

Immediately after doing it I felt so ugly. I knew I had made a grave mistake. I thought, "Oh my, what have I done!" Not only was it super ugly, the perm split down the middle. This meant my mom's hair stylist had to cut it out and redo it. Yes I lied to her too and told her this was okay by my mom! Everyone thought I was a little boy, from customers at our restaurant to students and teachers at my new school. People would come up to me and say, "Son do you play ball?"

I was horrified and I looked hideous! As you can see from these pictures, this was the serious state of my emotions and probably even more so being at such a young, delicate age! I always say the day my grandfather died I went from eight years old to thirty years old in the blink of an eye! I felt like I became the parent of two, a man and woman who I called mom and dad. I no longer allow my emotions to get the best of me and do anything too drastic because boy can they make you ugly!

## STAYING CURRENT

I think the hardest thing in the world to do it to keep up with the times and trends! It is very hard to keep your appearance current and not feel like you have become outdated and stagnant unless you stay classic. I tend to always stay moderately classic so that I can wear things for years and also mix and match accordingly. It is a little harder with shoes, but it can be done. I keep my shoes also because what goes out of style must come in style again! So I am not being a proponent of hoarding, but hold on to your favorite goodies as you can have a few cycles of wearing them.

When it comes to makeup and hair trends they also come and go. It is fun to experiment, but remember there is a work friendly professional look and a Friday night look. Please don't blur the two as it is quite obvious. Professional = Polished. Not everyone even wears makeup and that is totally fine too, but always make sure to look clean, polished, and have your hair nicely groomed. This could mean a nice short haircut or nicely blown hair. Polished means effort which in turn will keep you looking and feeling good about yourself because you were mindful

about your appearance. This matters because it is a reflection of who you are and how you are feeling. Are you a mess or a success? Only you are in charge of showing the world that!

When it comes to looking (and feeling) your best, you will need to be prepared to face the world with your best self. And the best way to do this is to load your closet with the key essentials for success. These items will make up the basics of your wardrobe and having them ready to wear will eliminate time and stress when preparing to take on your day! Here are some tips that can help you make some really empowering choices without having to buy a million things but they will also help make you and your wardrobe stand out and look polished!

# Your Wardrobe Essentials

There are three components to making up an article of clothing that would be considered "essential." First, it has to be versatile, meaning the more it works with the rest of your wardrobe, the more versatile it is. These items tend to be monochromatic and neutral in color and can work with multiple outfit options. For instance, the perfect blazer can be worn with jeans, black dress pants, a mid length pencil skirt and/ or a cute party dress. The versatility of the blazer makes it a perfect wardrobe essential.

Second, the item needs to be of exceptional quality. The fabric itself needs to be of high end quality to not only ensure the longevity of the item, but also the style of the piece tends to look so much better as it's a high end item. People will notice this and it will also increase how good you feel about yourself when wearing it.

And third, a wardrobe essential should be a classic. That perfect little black dress or a nice fitting pair of jeans. These are examples of classic

items that you will be able to wear again and again and knock it out of the park every time. The color black is another example of a classic wardrobe essential. When an item is black it tends to be flattering on everyone, stains are hard if not impossible to see, and it makes the perfect basic to add any color you wish, so you are able to have fun with prints or other colorful accessories.

Here are some key examples of items that are considered perfect wardrobe essentials to add to your closet:

- Little Black Dress
- Black Blazer
- White button down shirt with collar
- Black trousers
- Knee length pencil skirt
- Classic style trench coat
- Black Leather bag/purse
- Blue Jeans
- 1 Pair of black and 1 Pair of nude pumps
- White and/or Black cardigan sweaters
- Set of pearls
- Diamond studs…or cubics!

# *Beauty*

## WHEN TO DITCH YOUR MASCARA!

When it comes to make up and beauty products, as much as we want them to last a lifetime, they sadly have an expiration date. It is key that you pay attention to when you should throw away beauty products and cosmetics so you do not put yourself at risk for any unwanted bacteria or skin irritations that may occur.

### *MASCARA:*

Eye makeup is especially vulnerable to bacteria, so after three months of using your favorite eye lash enhancer, throw it out and replace it with a brand new one. Same goes for eye liner, and eye primers.

### *LIP GLOSSES & LIPSTICKS:*

These are also items that although we may LOVE, we cannot hang on to for over 12 months. Usually lip products that have gone past their expiration date develop an odor or scent that is unmistakably like what you may remember your grandma's lipstick to smell like. In either case, after 12 months throw it out and replace it with a new one, and maybe even try out a new color to mix up your makeup routine!

### *FOUNDATION:*

Foundation and skin care are items that you need to pay extra attention to. Our skin is the largest organ and we need to ensure we are taking good care of it. Most foundations and skin care products have a shelf life of 12 months, but just make sure by checking on the

packaging. Foundations do not permeate a scent like lip products do once they've gone bad, so pay attention to the texture of the makeup if it is unclear as to when you bought it or if you haven't kept track of how long you've had it. If it has separated and looks thick or clumpy when it was once smooth and silk-like, chances are it has gone past it's expiration date.

## *BRUSHES*:

Makeup Brushes must be cleaned. Use a brush cleaner and wash them with shampoo and conditioner, then spray them with alcohol especially if you have been sick.

Fever Blisters are dangerous. Be very conscious if you are prone to getting them not to reuse the lipstick you were using during the course of the fever blister. Chop off the contaminated area and spray with alcohol. Personally I usually chuck them if I have had a fever blister. I also do not use my makeup brushes anywhere near a fever blister to be safe. In those moments I use my hands and cotton swabs.

## WHEN TO NIX YOUR NAIL PRODUCTS!

## *NAIL POLISH:*

Nail products that have passed their expiration can spread bacterial and fungal infections that may cause risks to your health. Pay good attention to their shelf life and keep your eye out for signs of spoilage. Separation and/or a clumpy, unspreadable consistency are key signs that your polish has gone off.

## *NAIL TOOLS:*

Nail clippers and cuticle cutters are both items that can be purchased in stainless steel, therefore they are able to last for quite some time without having to replace them, which can be expensive to do. Just make sure to keep these items clean and sanitary by soaking them in 99% alcohol after each use. Nail files and buffers are slightly different as they cannot be cleaned and just need to be thrown away and then replaced. A good rule of thumb on this is every 3-4 weeks if using often.

## WHEN TO ZAP YOUR ZIT CREAM!

## *BLEMISH CREAMS/SKIN CARE:*

Aside from causing skin irritation and possible burning or discomfort, and expired pimple treatment cream won't do anything as it has lost it's ability to actually remove the zit and heal the problem. It also poses as a bacteria risk and could worsen the already problematic area. These treatments need to be stored in a cool and dry place to ensure it's efficiency and needs to be replaced every 8-12 months.

## THE BEST TIP YET

Confidence can dress you up better than the most expensive clothes, makeup, hair, and shoes in the world! To exude confidence shows and exemplifies a rich inner life that is yours, that you own, and that no one can take away from you! I would much rather spend time with a confident person who knows a thing or two, then a good looking shallow and insecure person who may have on really expensive stuff, but is poor spiritually and internally. How about you? Do you feel

confident in yourself? What changes do you need to make in yourself and in your personal style to reflect how you want to appear?

# I Want More

I remember once upon a time thinking (and not too long ago by the way), "Do I want to be in this position next year in my life?" The answer was no. Absolutely not! So what did I do about it?

I knew I needed to do more for myself. I needed to dress and look the way I wanted to be treated—the way I wanted to feel. I needed to put more effort into the way I looked so people would treat me better and with more respect. I was the only one who could do this for me.

It was hard. I had to be my own cheerleader, and for a long season my own accountability partner. I made small moves in the right direction every day until I started seeing results, and you can too! Here are some questions I asked myself to advance my Appearance RESET:

1. What am I doing today to move my life upward? Am I falling forward in faith or am I flying forward in faith? Its okay as long as its forward.

2. What can I do to be more abundant and take chances? How can I extend myself to better my appearance, even if for a moment? Am I being an imposter to my feelings?

3. Are there things I need to do in my life to get more organized? How can I be sure I will not appear frazzled and my energy and appearance will look balanced, polished, and strong.

4. Do I write down my appearance goals? Are they clear to me? Are they obtainable or ridiculous?

5. How do I see myself dressed in my future role? How can I dress so I look like I belong in the life I want? When I look the part it helps me believe I will get there.

*"Be conscious and mindful of your sweet heart for it too is like that of a beautiful flower that can wilt or bloom depending how you care for it."*

—JJ

I am in the best shape of my life spiritually and physically. I am happy. I am balanced. I have taken control of my life. **My outsides match my insides.** I now have a real relationship with God and it shows as I am able to stop the crazy and continue to fall and fly forward in faith. I was capable of change and you are too. The choice is yours. How hard are you willing to work for it? It is time for you to let your appearance experience a RESET. Let your light shine and show the world your fabulous self. Happy is the secret to beautiful!

*"You're beautiful from head to toe, my dear love.*
*Beautiful beyond compare, absolutely flawless."*

—Song of Songs 4:7, The Message Bible

## Chapter Nine

# RESET—Faith

*"Hope is the breath of fresh air God breathes into our souls. Hope is the heartbeat of our spirits that enriches our lives. Hope whispers, 'Try another time,' and renews our strength to keep going."*

—JJ

One day it became abundantly clear to me that without a real relationship with God, I had no hope. If I had no hope then I had nothing, and so I started my search!

I needed to know if God was real, and if He was real did He care about me. I had heard about God all my life, but I couldn't say that I had any kind of a personal relationship with Him ... or if that was even possible. In the middle of all my other RESETs, it suddenly became important to me that I do a little soul searching and find out about my own spirituality.

### Faith Thermometer
#### Figure 9.1

**I Am All In**
*I love God with all my heart,*
*He is always with me*

**I Trust God**
*He guides my steps, I hear His voice*

**I Know God Loves Me**
*I believe He cares about me personally,*
*I try to hear His voice*

**I Look For God**
*I want a closer relationship, but often feel far away*

**I Believe in God**
*I think He is good & benevolent, my faith is general*

**Is God Real?**
*I question God, but wish I could believe …*
*"Where are You?"*

**I Don't Believe in God**
*I am on my own, it is up to me*

**Where I Am Now**                    **Where I Want To Be**

On the "Where I Am Now" thermometer, mark the category which best fits your level of belief and relationship with God. Do you desire a Faith RESET?

Now take a look at the "Where I Want to Be" thermometer and consider where you would like to find yourself in the future. A Faith RESET is the easiest of all because God meets you and brings you close to His side!

## Questions for Faith

1. Did you ever have faith in God?

2. If so, when did you lose your faith in God? (Was it because you felt like He failed you … an event or trauma, grief, disappointment, death of a loved one, illness, etc.?)

3. At what time in your life did you ever feel like anything and everything was possible and you believed it could happen because God was with you?

4. Do you desire a relationship with God? Do you wish you had stronger faith?

5. In what ways are you developing your faith and growing in your relationship with God?

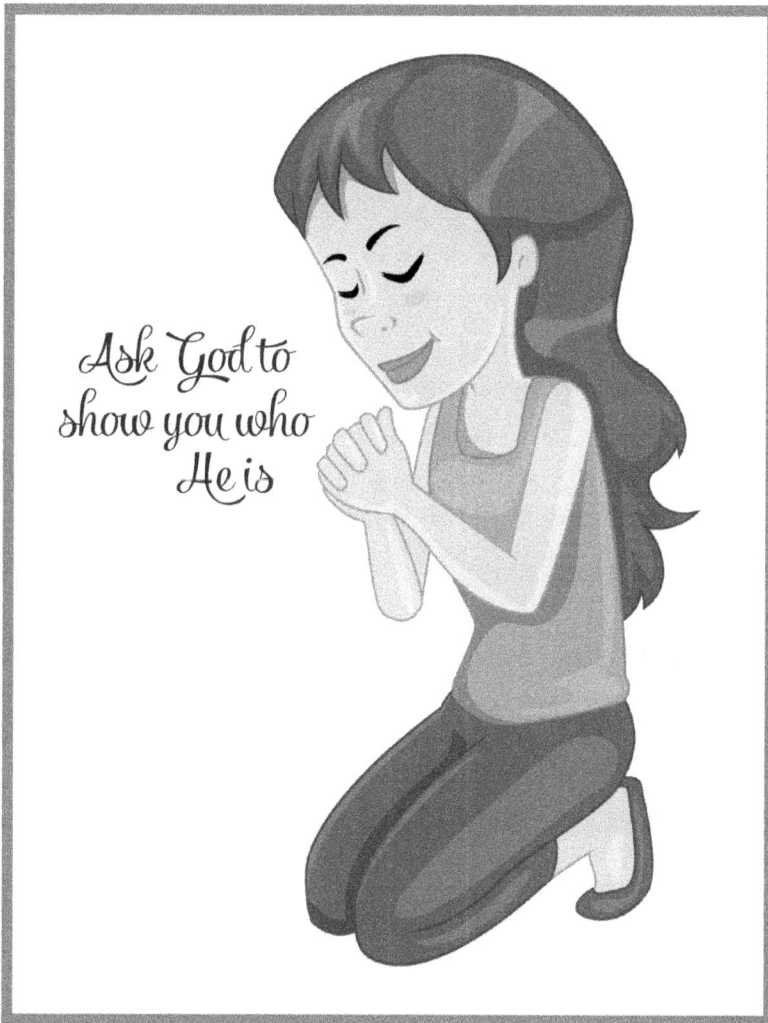

Ask God to show you who He is

I remember the day I officially met the Holy Spirit. The voice was clear. It said, "Call your mother," and for once in my life, I acted immediately. I knew this prompt to call my mom was serious. This call was when I found out about all the money my then boyfriend, now ex-boyfriend was borrowing from her for years without my knowledge. All that money. Gone! I was dumbfounded. God knew my mom needed to hear from me that day. He knew I needed to learn the truth and face reality.

God was talking to me, and it was about time I started listening. He was saving me from a hard life. He had a purpose for me. It was time to live that call on my life and stop wasting time chasing all the wrong things.

I believed in God. I believed the Bible was God's Word, yet I wasn't really living it. Looking back I realize I always have had one foot in with God and one foot out in the world. I sometimes wondered if God forgot about me or if He was on a very long lunch break! I knew all these experiences I was having could not be the plans He had for me—all these RESETS. What was the point of all this pain?

*Maybe God was too busy dealing with other people's problems to tend to mine ...*

"Maybe God is too busy dealing with other people's real problems to tend to my small problems in comparison," I thought. Then I almost felt guilty asking for help. Let's face it, was my sad love life and business disappointments as important as someone who is sick, hungry, or losing their home? So I figured I could handle things on my own, better off not to bother God with the small stuff. Every once in a while when things just felt out of control I would ask God, "Why? Why me? What did I do to deserve this? I try

to be a good person! Can you please help me? Can you fix this? Please? Is being kind a sin that I have to deal with being taken advantage of? Is being loving detrimental?" Let's face it: both outcomes were so painful. There didn't appear to be any upside in the moments of my RESET … until I realized yes, there was!

I grew up Catholic. In my upbringing, the teachings were focused on the fear of God not the love of God. I had very strong faith—I didn't waver in my belief about God, but looking back my relationship with God was not very strong. My faith was strong, but my relationship was weak. It was one-sided. I kept getting signs from God, and it became abundantly clear that I needed to know His Son, Jesus. I prayed to know Him better and a few weeks later, I met a person on an airplane. She was a music manager coming back from a show. I felt very comfortable because we both worked in entertainment. Somehow we got into a very deep conversation. Eventually I told her about my Jesus dilemma and she said, "I am a pastor."

"Really!" I said, "You in that gorgeous leopard coat … you're a pastor? Seriously?"

"Yes," she answered, "and if you want to know Jesus and get closer to God, you met the right girl. I was just like you and my life has been forever changed!"

I will never forget that conversation. It was the beginning of me having a deeper relationship with the Lord and knowing who He is.

Maybe you didn't grow up around faith of any kind. Maybe your parents only religion was sports on Sundays. I get it. Maya Angelou says, "We do better when we know better," so how are you to do if you do not know?

One of my favorite scriptures says that God knows the plans He has for us and those plans are meant for our good. How can you believe there are plans if you don't really believe in God? What if you don't know God? What if you don't hear God's voice or even know that He has one?

I can understand the struggle, but think about this. We cannot see the blood running through our brains, but it is there. We cannot see the oxygen we breath, but it is there. We cannot see the wind, but it is there. So just because we cannot see God does not mean He is not there. There is way more evidence of God than you could ever imagine once you set out to discover Him!

> *"Ask and it will be given to you; seek and you will find; knock and the door will be opened to you."*
>
> Matthew 7:7

If you have never ever thought much about God, or you have no clue how on earth to have a relationship with Him, then I encourage you now to start seeking God. It is literally as simple as asking Him to reveal Himself to you. He will. He knows what kind of proof you need that He exists, that He loves you, and wants the best for you. He will answer you. He will talk to you through strangers, through billboards and signs, through music, through nature, through things you read. Just try it. Ask Him to prove He's listening and then pay attention. He'll answer.

As you build your relationship with Him, you will be filled with hope, love, mercy and grace. Hope starts an internal dialogue that breeds faith. If you have a continual dialogue with God you will become enlightened and the people in your life will be encouraged by your uplifting spirit!

So how do we grow our spiritual muscles and give them the nutrition they need? How do we get closer to God or how do we find Him if we do not know Him?

We all want immediate results when we pray and if we don't get them, we figure maybe God is not going to help so why bother? We may think that since He forgives everyone anyway, He will forgive us too. We might decide we should live our lives however we want because we only live once, right?

But you know this isn't right. At some point in the still of the night, in the quiet, when the vibration of life has settled, you feel the uncertainty, you still have the questions: Who am I? What am I doing with my life? Why am I here? What is my purpose?

We are connected to God and each other. That longing in us is our soul's GPS system searching to connect with God—our source of life! Yes our soul, our spirit, our authentic self is missing out. It wants balance, it wants nutrition, it wants to be its true divine self, and connected to God as He intended.

Take a step back. Reflect on where you are right now. Is your faith in need of a RESET? Mine was. Through all my other RESETs, I didn't realize that I was searching for a relationship with God all along. Every other RESET was good, but somehow still empty, not quite complete. When I began to seek God—invite Him to be an active part of my life—all the other RESETs suddenly took on new meaning. I had greater fulfillment. I had joy! I want you to experience this too.

> *"Sometimes you only have a word from*
> *God but a word from God is enough"*
>
> —T.D. Jakes

Sit still and let yourself Heal

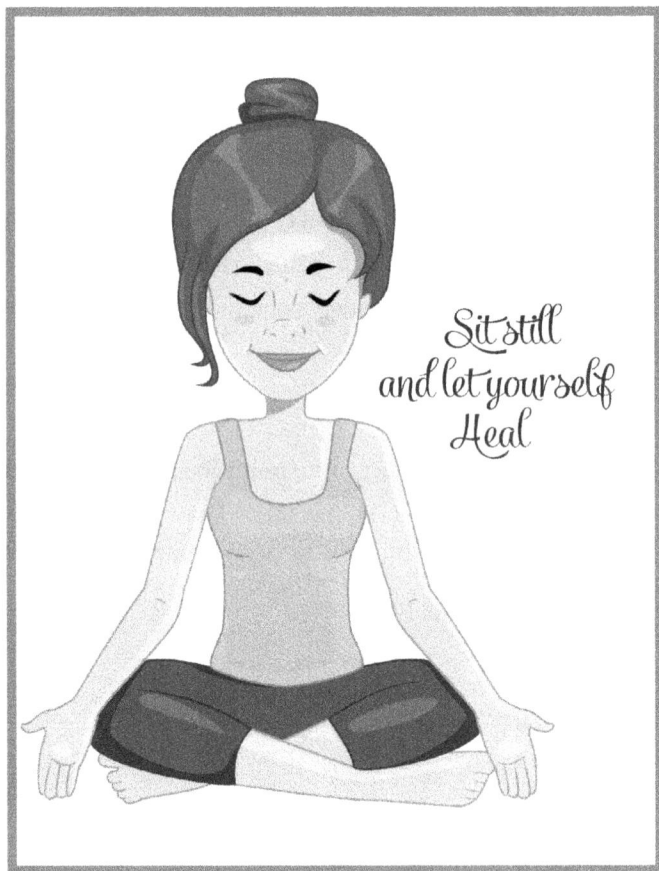

When you die can you look God in the eye? This is something I started to think about a lot during my RESETs. Was I living the life God had intended for me? When I died could I meet my Maker and say I was proud of how I lived my life? I was proud about some things, and I wasn't proud about others and I needed to figure out why and how I could do better. I knew there was a better life than that of what I was living. I needed a new perspective. I mostly lived my life one day to the next, in fear, easily distracted, not sure of where I was going. I was always busy and that usually meant I forgot all about God until I was in some kind of mess and needed to be rescued.

I now look for opportunities to connect with God in the midst of my activities, rather than just letting life push me around and trying to catch up with Him when I get everything else done. I try to be aware of what He is presenting to me, what He is offering me. Whenever I spend time in His presence, He makes everything clear. When I obey Him, He blesses me and lets me walk in His favor.

Things do not always come as I hoped or saw them in my head, but surely (and sometimes way too slowly) they do come. This is all part of that surrender that I oh, so struggle with. No matter who you are it is hard to be still and listen. I have learned though that it is in the quiet times with God that I get my answers and gifts of creativity. Be still and heal! This is not easy, but a necessary practice. Prayer and meditation is better than any medicine you can get your hands on … and its free!

*"Now faith is confidence in what we hope for and assurance about what we do not see. This is what the ancients were commended for. By faith we understand that the universe was formed at God's command, so that what is seen was not made out of what was visible."*
—Hebrews 11:1-3

People often lose their faith when they feel like God has abandoned or failed them. It's like, "Hey God, did you leave the building? Hello! Where are you?" When I felt like this, I realized it was because my spiritual muscles were weak. I was not feeding my spirit the proper nutrition and I felt it! I tried other things to make me feel better, but I found out wine is not an elixir for healing, it is only one for pleasure or avoidance of reality. My spirit was very heavy and it showed inside and

outside. Of all the areas where I needed a RESET, my spirit needed it the most.

# Spiritual Weight Loss

Just as I had needed physical weight loss, I now needed spiritual weight loss. Just like I needed to build strong muscles in my body, I needed to build my spiritual muscles so I could become spiritually strong. To be truly healthy—body, soul, spirit and mind—I needed to find my true faith and purpose again. True faith feels like the warm embrace by someone you love. It is an all encompassing knowing that in this moment everything is perfect. It is a beautiful peaceful feeling that stays with you. It resonates in your heart and soul and dances in there—beautifully swirling around reminding you that you are indeed loved.

Building your spiritual muscles and losing spiritual weight is no different than traditional muscle building and weight loss. It just requires a different perspective. The first thing to consider is this:

1. What nutrition are you feeding your spirit to build your spiritual muscles?

2. Who are your friends?

3. Does the person you love have a spiritual practice? Do they even believe in God, and do they support your beliefs?

4. What are you listening to?

5. What do you watch on tv?

6. What are you reading?

7. What kind of conversations are you having with others or yourself?

8.  Are these things serving you in a higher way or a negative way?

What you feed grows! What are you feeding yourself spiritually? Take a look at your life and you will know. The scripture says, "Therefore, since we are surrounded by such a huge crowd of witnesses to the life of faith, let us strip off every weight that slows us down, especially the sin that so easily trips us up. And let us run with endurance the race God has set before us." God wants us to cast our cares on Him and let Him care for us. When we do this it is spiritual weight loss.

Hope & Grace are friends ...
more than that, they are family!

Our faith is often shaken when the people we love hurt us. It can be a spouse, lover, friend, family member, or coworker. Hurt is hurt and it is painful, period. God pours His grace out on us. This grace allows us to have compassion and love for those who have hurt us. Hope reminds us that there are better things ahead. It gives us courage to continue on, even when things are hard. I have loved hard and lost hard. Grace and hope have carried me through.

I went through a lot and thought, "Where was God?" I went through more and thought, "I need God." I went through more still and thought, "I love God." I went through even more and said, "Thank you, God!" My surrender finally allowed me to see all that I was protected, spared, and saved from. Going through it I didn't understand. Getting through it and having clarity gave me my sight. Gratitude, love and truth is the essence of my vibration now.

## TRUST + ACCEPTANCE + SURRENDER = GRACE

For God's grace granted me divine love, for God's grace made me seek Him. For God's grace changed me forever!

> *"For it is by grace you have been saved,*
> *through faith—and this is not from*
> *yourselves, it is the gift of God."*
> — Ephesians 2:8

# Let it Go

When we are children we feel like anything and everything is possible. We have not been tainted by the world yet and we still feel and remember God. Our lives are hopeful and our memories are short! When we are children we don't hold on to things. We just go on to the

next thing. We let things go easily and therefore we are free. As adults life becomes cumbersome, full of burdens and responsibilities until we are heavy. If we fall, we think about it way too much and often only get halfway up if that. Embarrassment, shame, and fear keep us from trying again, we prefer to play it safe, but there is no value in the safety as it stunts our growth. This is not what God wants for us. Sometimes life doesn't work out like we planned. Sometimes we make bad choices and fall down, then we question God and push Him out of our heart— right when we need Him most!

*"Guard your heart above all else for it
determines the course of your life."*

—Proverbs 4:23

*"Don't answer God with a question mark when
He tells you with an exclamation point!"*

—JJ

Letting go starts as an exercise in faith. We must let go of all the things that do not serve us. We must let go of all the things in our life that hurt us. God gives us the courage and wisdom to let go of these things, to surrender them to Him and know that He has something better for us. While you wait for the better thing to come, trust Him. He has good things for you and you will never be able to step into those if you keep carrying around all this excess baggage—this spiritual fat. Let it go!

I have had to let go of dreams of what could have been. I spent years pursuing some dreams and letting go of them was hard. As I did that, I made room to birth new ones, but still God was like, "Not so fast, Jacqui, you need to wait! You have a lot to learn!"

I was hurt, and hurt people hurt people, period! Before I could move forward with my faith RESET, I first had to totally let go and forgive those who had hurt me. Most of all, I had to forgive myself. Once I did, my spiritual weight loss got a real jump start! Forgiveness set off a chain reaction in me and I was able to remember things without inflicting new pain. I even found gratitude in the memory. Forgiveness propels us forward in walking in our truth. Forgiving others sets us free. By forgiving I finally broke the shackles and set aside the weight I was carrying on my spirit.

## FORGIVENESS = FREEDOM!

*"You are a mighty person in the making, a
masterpiece in progress, a miracle in motion."*
—Tim Storey

# Walking in Victory

I believe in miracles. I believe in God's Word and I am not afraid
because I believe in what God is doing in my life. I have optimism
because my faith is strong. I do not let people speak to my situation
or implode it with fear. I speak to God and I let Him speak to my
situation. By doing this I rise. I walk in victory—no matter what my
present circumstance, I know I will win.

We will never walk in victory and relish in all the gifts that God has
in store for us if we don't grow our spiritual muscles and show courage
in our faith! We need to be lions, we need to roar! We have God behind
us so what is there to be afraid of really? If God is for us who can be
against us? I can do all things through Christ who strengthens me.

The more I got to know God the more I wanted to know God. The
more I sought God the more it seemed crazy things would happen in
my life to flip it upside down. When you do strength training, you
grow your muscles through resistance training. Lifting weights sculpts
those muscles. God used all those crazy things—that resistence—to
build and sculpt my spiritual muscles. God likes to use those people
others don't expect greatness from and turn them into great testaments
of faith to glorify His name!

# Walking in Love

*"To love oneself is the beginning
of a lifelong romance."*

—Oscar Wilde

Lack of self love affects everything in your life! Growing up I was taught to love others, be kind to others, but looking back I was never taught about the inward journey. I was never taught to be kind to myself, to love me. I personally don't know many people who were. Maybe they just instinctively got it, I did not!

*"Hope deferred makes the heart sick, but
a longing fulfilled is a tree of life."*

—Proverbs 13:12

You know how it feels when you are in love and someone is devoting all this attention to you and you to them, it is so beautiful! You feel so good about yourself and your life, and you are hopeful! In those moments we are at peace because the person we love, loves us! All seems right in the world. Unfortunately, that feeling is dependent on someone else. If that ends and we don't feel on top of the world anymore, how do we rebuild our crushed spirits? How do we find hope again?

Each time we are hurt by another person it seems to hurt a little worse. The older we become, the more conscious we are and the pain is deeper. We become sad, stuck, and less optimistic. We lose our hope.

During my faith RESET, I turned to God. I started reading the Bible more, meditating everyday, always praying and learning the power of

surrender. Most of all, I began trusting God's timing. I learned to prune away the negative chatter to blossom a beautiful new song to myself!

*"When the time is right, I the Lord*
*will make it happen."*
—Isaiah 60:22

The first step to my inward journey of faith was to quit giving my power away. I asked myself these questions:

1. Why do I not feel qualified?

2. Why do I think someone is my end all be all?

3. Why do I think they are going to save the day or elevate me and my spirit, or my business in some way?

4. Shouldn't I be able to do this for myself? I know I used too. What happened?

5. When did I get caught up in codependency?

*"Delight yourself in the Lord and he will*
*give you the desires of your heart."*
—Psalm 37:4

Faith

Belief

Strengthen your
muscles of FAITH
and BELIEF
so you can squash
FEAR!

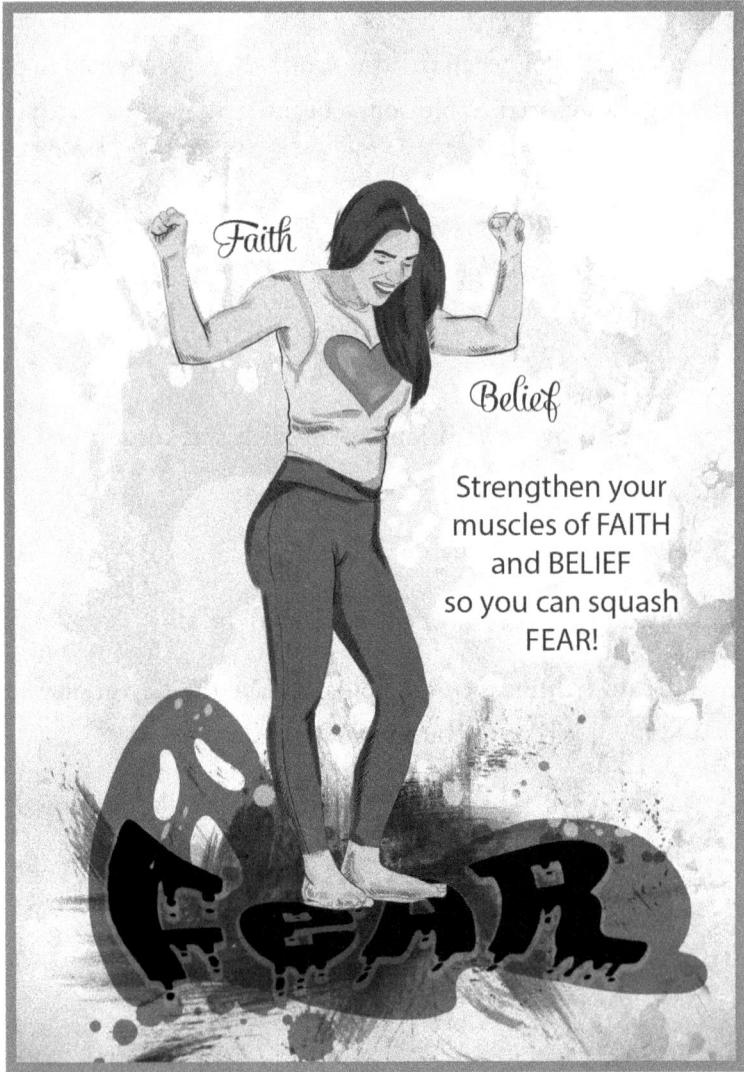

I am a testimony to listen to those desires God puts in your heart because if He plants the seed He will grow the roots and bloom the tree. It just may not be the way you thought but it will be better than you ever imagined. In the journey I did not feel qualified to write books, do makeup on celebrities, or host tv and radio shows. I did not feel that I belonged in the positions of what I was doing and then I learned that it doesn't matter if I think I am qualified or not or what

anyone else thinks for that matter. It simply doesn't matter because it is God that qualifies us. He gives us the resources, the wisdom, and the support team to make it happen. Now when someone tries to put me down, devalues me, and tries to steal my joy I take serious note never to share a dream again with them and thank God for exposing that person to me. I note them as dangerous as if I allowed their negativity into my space they could hinder my success. I have been spoken over by God so I have value as I have been spoken over by the divine! He is our original parent, so I know He will always protect me!

*"Don't let your light shine in darkness,*
*let your light shine with greatness."*

—JJ

# Walking with the Right People

So how do I create an extraordinary life that is aligned with God and the right people that will nurture growth?

Play in life with people who are positive, who love God, who have your best interest at heart to always have faith in you and root for your success in all areas of your life. Don't play in the dark with people who bring you down, talk behind your back, and give criticism you didn't ask for. Life is a process, don't you want to play with people who will enjoy it with you with a smile and a loving word of encouragement? God shows you who people are. Listen to Him, He will protect you. He will align you with the right people and when you have to make big decisions find your anchor in God. When you know the plans He has for you are good, you know how the story ends—you can relax a bit about the details. That takes faith.

# *Love Conquers All*

*"Do not let your hearts be troubled. You have faith
in God; have faith also in me. In my Father's house
there are many dwelling places ... If I go and prepare
a place for you, I will come back again and take
you to Myself, so that where I am you also may be
... Peace I leave with you; My peace I give to you
... Do not let your hearts be troubled or afraid."*

—John 14

If we all took a minute each day with gratitude and paid attention to the gifts we receive—large or small—we would be amazed at how God works in our lives each day. I can honestly now say that God is the center of my life! God is love, so love is the center of how I operate my life. Love is the vibration I operate on. If we all made Love our center, the world would be a better place and so would we.

I invite you to RESET your faith today. Of all the RESETs, this is by far the most the valuable. A relationship with God will open up treasures untold for you. Your life will take on new meaning, new direction. Hope will rise and love like you have never before known will wrap Himself around you and change everything ... absolutely everything!

*"Now these three remain: faith, hope and
love. But the greatest of these is love."*

—1 Corinthians 13:13

## Chapter Ten

# Walking in Wisdom

*"The gift of wisdom is the pearls that God wraps around*
*you to enlighten you with His kindness and discernment."*

—JJ

*"But the wisdom that comes from heaven is first of all*
*pure; then peace-loving, considerate, submissive, full*
*of mercy and good fruit, impartial and sincere."*
—James 3:17 NIV

*"If any of you lacks wisdom, you should ask*
*God, who gives generously to all without finding*
*fault, and it will be given to you."*
—James 1:5 NIV

By now you are either on your journey towards RESET or you are totally RESET! You are the bright light that shines into the lives of others, you are like the ambient noise that whispers in the hearts of those you love and puts a smile on their faces. You are a gift to all those you encounter. You are joy, you are peace, you are love and you are God's child. Let your divine light shine always. Don't forget there is power in the pause. There is always a time for discernment, time to seek divine guidance, and time for wise decision making. When you rest in the Lord He will restore you.

I have one final exercise that I want you to hold dear and use all the days of your life. I want you to give yourself a heart x-ray often. When you are finally feeling something strong I want you to sit quietly and meditate and pray about it and feel your feelings. Feel your thoughts. Ask yourself why and surrender to them. Release them if they don't serve you. Now imagine yourself taking them off our heart—like you would take something off a shelf—and hand them to God. Give all your problems to God's helping hands for all your joy!

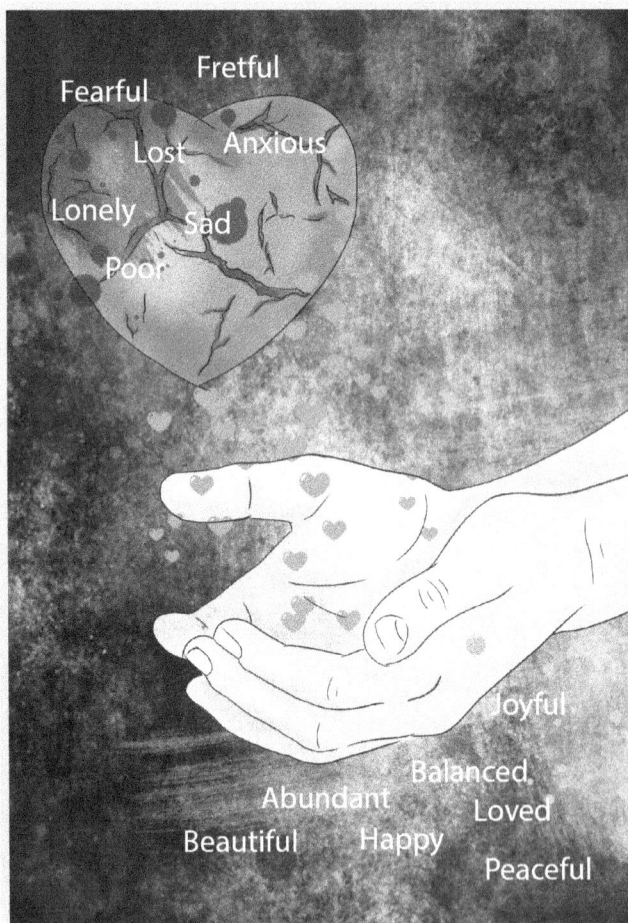

I thought I wanted normal all my life, and then I realized I wanted extraordinary. I wanted the kind of extraordinary that comes from knowing God! I identify most with Jeremiah from the Bible. Like him, I too suffered from much rejection but had endless faith. I was honest with God when it came to my despair and how tired I was of all the opposition. I too felt hopeless at times, but I knew I wasn't because I had faith and that I was blessed with the grace of endurance to keep going! Endurance is key to be successful in your RESET. You have to have the faith that God will continue to lead your steps. You have to trust that to be true! Keep the light of Christ burning in your life! If you want great things then you need to make great sacrifices in order to realize great achievements.

> *"Listen with your heart, think with your mind, and make your decisions with God."*
>
> —JJ

My RESETs were not in vain. The effort gave me the confidence in myself to keep going and stand on my own two feet! It is never too late to RESET. Sometimes we need more than one RESET, but each time the process takes us closer to where we long to be.

God is love. He teaches us with love and shows us how to walk in faith. As you recognize His love for you, you will learn to love yourself, and that lets you offer the world the very best you! You steer in the direction of your focus, so if you keep looking up, you will go upwards. If you keep looking forward (not to your past), then you will go forward. Sometimes I like to think, "What's at the end of my rainbow?" Then I work backwards from there. Sometimes it is just easier to figure it out that way. God has a way of telling us the direction we are supposed to take or be led in, but it is up to us to listen. Listen with your heart, think with your mind, and make your decisions with God.

I know I am RESET because I make decisions that I don't always want to make, but I do anyway. Because they will serve my higher good, my RESET brain wants to make these good decisions, therefore she does. I do believe in fairytales and miracles. I wish I could end this book like a fairytale, wouldn't that be fun? I would end it telling you that I finally found my true love and that I ran off happily ever after with my soul mate ... but I can't do that just yet. I will in due time.

Love is the greatest gift in life—to love and be loved. I pray I will soon experience a true divine love. I know God will give me that gift. In the meantime, I have been focusing forward in faith and kicking butt for God ... and for me! That is a miracle in itself: to be afforded the opportunity to RESET into a new life. God is good.

RESET is about you, not about resetting someone else. It is about surrender, letting go and forging forward in your new path. No matter what other people are doing to you or to themselves, you will always have equanimity inside you. Choose you, choose God. It is the only way of peace and success. Serenity brings creativity which in retrospect centers oneself. Breaking up with a dream to go after another is the hardest part of the trek on the destination, but if you want room for greatness there must be enough room for it to enter. Let it!

*Choose you.*
*Choose God.*

When you are walking in your RESET, you will have learned the power of perception. When you feel a problem arising, practice looking at the four walls of the illusion of a problem. Walk around it, pause and pray about it. Use discernment. Don't be in a rush, but let God reveal the truth to you. Speak to God about the situation and let Him speak to you.

My hope is that RESET has inspired you as it inspired me to take my life back. I hope you use your RESET to continue to free yourself of the shackles and burdens (often internal) and by facing them you will be set free. I want you to soar like an eagle. Be sly as a serpent and soft as a dove. Live in your truth. Fulfill your unique purpose. Dance in the sun and most of all let your light shine bright like the star you are.

This is your movie—its that thing called life. How do you want it to play out? Are you viewing your life from high atop the mountain with certainty and strength in God or are you viewing it with fear which is false evidence appearing real? You can make as many edits as you want so RESET and REWARD yourself with a great life.

God will give it to you but he won't let you keep it unless you do the right things to deserve it.

Strength is a virtue. It is good to be strong and independent. Strength can also be a curse. That same independence can keep you from letting the people you need come close. It can keep you from asking for help or accepting help even when offered. Be open to encouraging people that show up to help you. They are a gift.

It recently dawned on me that this year I have six books coming out, I am a Certified Professional Life Coach, Master Business Coach, the executive producer, creator, and host of my own show, I have written and released a wonderful children's song and I have collaborated with a fabulous magazine. Wow, God is good! God, Jesus, and the Holy Spirit were my co-collaborators for all of this. There is no way it would have happened, because I am not that cool. I accepted the help that so kindly came my way all in the time I needed it. I truly listened and acted with childlike blind faith. I am completely aware that I am a conduit of His Spirit, I am humbled to be chosen, and I give God all the glory because when my human brain thinks about it, its ridiculous that I am writing a children's animated book series! But when my soul considers it, it makes absolute sense because I identify with all the feelings and resonate with all the lessons portrayed on each journey of each story that I write. Go it alone? Never. I am strong, resourceful and independent, yet totally in need of God and others.

Sit back, reflect, and then rejoice. Don't let the naysayers plant seeds of doubt or shame in you. No matter how RESET you are, these seeds can make you feel undeserving. Shut this out. Pause and reflect on who you are and how wonderful you are. Respect your journey and the progress you have made. If you feel unqualified, remember that it is God who qualifies you—because He is worthy and you are His, you are worthy too.

*"For we live by faith, not by sight."*
—2 Corinthians 5:7, NIV

Don't be moved by things you see, be moved by things you want to see. How do you know if you are RESET? How do you stay RESET? What if you need a RESET REFRESH? Now that you have the tools to deal with strongholds, negative thoughts, and limiting beliefs, a RESET REFRESH won't take as long. Each season will continue to propel you on a journey to your higher self. Each time leads to a more evolved, more powerful you. Each RESET elevates you to walk in a higher truth. Each RESET gives you wisdom. Each RESET makes you more fearless.

## Change Your Mind

If a thought doesn't feel good in my belly—in my soul—and if it upsets me, then I change it. It really is that simple and it changes everything. Our biggest asset in our RESET is our outlook, our perception, and

our tools. God gives us the strength to propel further. When we turn our troubles or questions to God first and ask for His help, He gives it. Your strength lies in your surrender to the Lord.

It is truly a divine experience when we change our thoughts to gratitude and allow the purity of wonder to flood our mind. It is beautiful to see the magic in the days and experience the present for what it is. I have my heart open again. I live with my soul open and let the Holy Spirit come through me and guide me. I have a heart to share with the world. After all this time I finally realized that I am working for God. I am listening to Jesus and I am trying to do good. I am here to help others. We all are. We touch people's lives everyday. It is the simple things we do that creates the magic of the human experience.

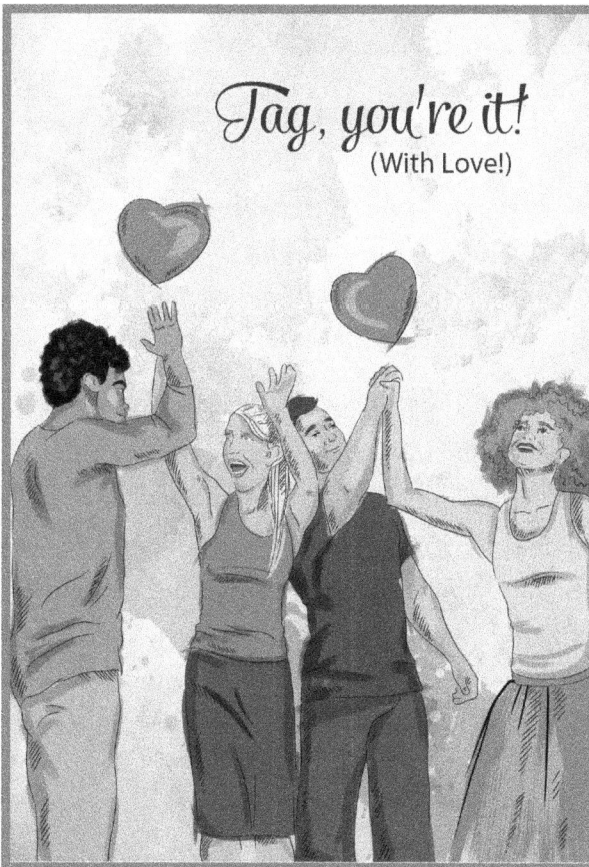

Tag, you're it!
(With Love!)

In my very animated imagination I see it as a domino effect. I touch someone and they touch someone and so on. So when we purely touch someone with love and kindness, then we leave them with that mark to do the same and transfer that energy to the next person. Its almost like playing tag … "You're it!" Now go touch someone and tag them with your love!

## Emotions Are Real

I was thinking long and hard during the writing of this book. Why do we have to struggle and have to have RESETs? Why can't we just live a happy life from the day we are born until the end? Sometimes it takes the bitter pain of an experience to propel us into a RESET before we truly learn. But then I thought, "Why does the pain have to linger so long and how can we wrap our minds around it to make the journey of the pain more understandable?"

Our emotions are real—we feel them. I mean we *really* feel this pain, but the emotions are not visible. We might see the response of an emotion, tears or angry words, but the emotion itself has not form or shape. The same can be said for a phantom limb.

I've been told that when someone has lost a limb, even though there is absolutely nothing there, the brain still feels pain in the missing limb. There is still a sensation that the arm or leg is there, even if completely gone. Some people have the feeling of a phantom limb for many years. Even after they have accepted the loss and their mind is in agreement that the limb is missing, pain still occurs. So why wouldn't the same thing be true for emotional loss. Can we not have the same phantom emotional pain where we still feel the presence of something lost in

our past, but still feel that pain or joy like it is still current? Can our phantom moments not represent the state we are in?

People call this an emotional attachment. Well, I've been there and it sure feels like *way* more than that. It does feel like you have lost a limb sometimes. The only way to relieve our phantom emotions is by two things. First, retrain your brain. Command it to live out a new story. Second, trust God. He was with you through the crisis and He is still with you now. He gave a free will to those who have hurt you, and their choices had consequences that affected you. He also gave you a free will to choose and those choices have had consequences. You still have that free will and the power to make a new choice, one that includes His protection and guidance. Step out of your past and into your present. Let your next steps be guided by the amazing possibilities of your future and do not give the past power over you any more.

We get ourselves in the most trouble when we make everything else our god. The first Commandment is "Thou shalt have no other god before Me." It may be that your "god" is constantly thinking of someone you love and they never leave your mind, or your "god" may be your job, or your possessions. Whatever has top priority becomes our idol. We put it before Him. Where is there room for God when he is taking a back seat? This never works.

I was in prayer and meditation one day during the suffering of my heartache with the loss of a friendship and I heard the words, "Seek His kingdom first and His righteousness and all these things will be given." Now I did not know that Bible verse at that time or if it even was one so I Googled it … and wouldn't you know, sure enough it is and it makes such perfect sense! When we seek God first we stay present, we have a relationship with Him and we have the chance to actually see what God is doing and can do in our lives. When we focus on all the other

things (which God calls idols), then we lose sight of the eternal love that is so important. By seeking God you are in a direct communion with what is good for you. When you don't, you are trying to control circumstances that are not in your control and it only leaves you breathless, upset, worried and most times disappointed. If we worried more about being right with God and less about being right, our lives would be better off. Most likely, it would take a miraculous turn.

The choices we make affect the rest of our lives. The older we get the more serious effects the choices have on us.

## SUCCESS = VICTORY

People who hurt you the most are those you expect the most from. Lose expectations from others and keep them for yourself and you will not get hurt like that. I have learned love is what matters the most. Our memories are our most valuable asset. This is the savings account I want to invest in because it will keep me rich, abundant, and joyful.

> *Hope breathes into the soul and whispers, "Try one more time!"*

Hope breathes into the soul and whispers, "Try one more time!" Hope breeds faith. Dr. Jerome Groopman, a hematologist-oncologist professor at the Harvard Medical School, published an entire book on the effects of hope and how powerful it is. It is called *The Anatomy of Hope: How People Prevail in the Face of Illness*. This book does not say that hope is an actual cure. It says, "Not that hope is sufficient for recovery, and not that strong religious convictions will triumph over disease, rather that hope and belief in the possibility of a cure, can give patients the courage to endure the severe side effects and complications inherent to the aggressive treatments required to effect a cure."

# RESET TIPS TO GO

- Always bring God in the room with you.

- Let people see God through you and in you.

- The more you get to know God and trust in Him, it displaces fear and worrying. Let Him transform you.

- Work on your inner beauty and your outer beauty will shine.

- If God can create an ocean, He can do anything in your life. So while you are in "the wait," let Him.

- Put energy into the people who put energy into you.

- Take a hint if you are always doing the chasing, stop. Turn around and go the other way so someone can chase you.

- Don't date someone during their recovery from their last relationship. Date them after they have come to a complete resolution, a clean ending, and are truly ready to begin again.

- Don't be moved by the things you see, but be moved by the things you want to see.

- Say the things you mean. Mean the things you say.

- Your wait will birth your win. When you wait for God and be strong in the wait, He will show you His goodness.

- Remember everything you need, you already have in you. God is in you. You are a child of God. He will provide. Quit freaking out.

I was on a plane once that I thought was going to go down. I wasn't crazy, when they started unloading gas and preparing for a crash landing, every passenger on the plane thought we were done for. In that moment I realized how small we are. We as individuals are just that. Yet we have life, and with that life we can make a difference. Some do, others do not. It is up to us to decide what type of life we shall lead, or we can just exist. But life is no longer than a whisper. So why not live to the fullest? Why not be the happiest you can be? Why not be the saddest you can be when you need to be? We landed safely and I got a second chance. I decided to really relish in my feelings and enjoy my existence to the best of my abilities.

Now you are RESET. Go live in bold fearlessness. Walk out your purpose. Fulfill your destiny. Explore your dreams and let God make them possible. Put God first and base your decisions on that relationship. Don't forget with God all things are possible—I am proof! You are reading my book which I never could have dreamed of on my own in a million years! So you see, miracles happen every day. You just read one! Until we meet again ...

Thank you for reading my book. With all my heart I love you ... may God bless YOU!

*"Delight yourself in the Lord and He will*
*give you the desires of your heart."*
—Psalm 37:4

Spread your *wings*

and *fly!*

# PRAYER OF PEACE

St. Francis of Assisi

*Lord, make me an instrument of thy peace.*
*Where there is hatred, let me sow love;*
*Where there is injury, pardon;*
*Where there is doubt, faith;*
*Where there is despair, hope;*
*Where there is darkness, light;*
*Where there is sadness, joy.*
*O Divine Master, grant that I may not so much seek.*
*To be consoled as to console,*
*To be understood as to understand,*
*To be loved as to love;*
*For it is in giving that we receive;*
*It is in pardoning that we are pardoned;*
*It is in dying to self that we are born to eternal life.*

# DO IT ANYWAY

Mother Teresa

*People are often unreasonable, illogical, and self-centered.* **Forgive them anyway.**

*If you are kind, people may accuse you of selfish ulterior motives.* **Be kind anyway.**

*If you are successful, you will win some false friends and some true enemies.* **Succeed anyway.**

*If you are honest and frank, people may cheat you.* **Be honest and frank anyway.**

*What you spend years building, someone could destroy overnight.* **Build anyway.**

*If you find serenity and happiness, they may be jealous.* **Be happy anyway.**

*The good you do today, people will often forget tomorrow.* **Do good anyway.**

*Give the world the best you have, and it may never be enough.* **Give the best you've got anyway.**

*You see, in the final analysis* **it is between you and God.**

**It was never between you and them anyway.**

# Let's Connect!

- Listen to RESET radio with host Jacqui Phillips & co-host Sifu Karl Romain or watch ResetUToday!

- Learn about The Adventures of Stushy & Bello!

- Learn how to become a certified RESET Coach!

- Invite Jacqui to speak at your event.

www.jacquiphillips.tv
www.resetUtoday.com

www.ingramcontent.com/pod-product-compliance
Lightning Source LLC
Chambersburg PA
CBHW070033100426
42740CB00013B/2682